Raising a Child With Arthritis

A PARENT'S GUIDE

This book has been provided to you by
the students of Brown Elementary
School and Upton Middle School.
St. Joseph, Michigan
In honor of their friends
Tanya Oatsvall and Stephen Dean.

Raising a Child With Arthritis

A PARENT'S GUIDE

AN OFFICIAL PUBLICATION OF
THE ARTHRITIS FOUNDATION

ATLANTA, GEORGIA

Published by the Arthritis Foundation
1330 West Peachtree Street
Atlanta, Georgia 30309

ISBN 0-912423-19-6

CONTENTS

ACKNOWLEDGMENTS ix
INTRODUCTION xi

PART ONE   **Juvenile Arthritis: A Primer** 1

    1   What Is Juvenile Arthritis? 3
        Diagnosis of Juvenile Arthritis 4
        Types of Juvenile Arthritis and Related Conditions 5

    2   Your Child's Health-Care Team 15
        How to Get the Most from Your Child's
        Medical Visits 16
          Specific Things to Tell the Doctor 20
          Specific Questions to Ask the Doctor 21

PART TWO   **Treatment Goals and Strategies** 26

    3   Medications 29
        Medication Guidelines 33
          Questions to Ask about Each Medication 34
        Saving Money on Medicines 35

    4   Physical Activity 37
        Exercise 37
        Posture 53
        Play and Recreational Activities 59

    5   Pain Assessment and Management 63
        What is Pain 63
        The Pain Puzzle 66
        Some Practical Approaches to Dealing with Pain . . 69
        Considering Alternative, Complementary and
        Unproven Remedies 74
          Questions to Ask about Complementary Treatments . . 76
          Be Suspicious of Any Treatment That 76

6 Office Procedures, Surgery and Hospitalization 77

Office Procedures 77

Surgery 78

*Questions to Ask the Doctor when Considering
Surgery* 79

7 Activities of Daily Living 83

Joint Protection 83

Making Daily Activities Easier 84

Diet and Nutrition 87

Calcium and Juvenile Arthritis 90

Eye Care 92

Dental Care 92

PART THREE **Living Well with Juvenile Arthritis** 95

8 Following the Medical Treatment Program 97

Helping Your Child Stick to the Plan 98

Discipline 100

Treatment Regimen Chart 102

9 Emotional and Social Adjustment 103

Staying in the Mainstream 103

What Siblings Are Thinking 107

More Help for Families 110

10 Growing Up with Arthritis 113

Ages and Stages 114

Making Friends 117

Sexuality 118

PART FOUR **Practical Matters of Living** 121

11 School Issues 123

Educating the Teachers 124

Sample Letter to Teacher 126

School Needs Checklist 128
Physical Education Activity Guide 132
Common School Concerns for Students with
Juvenile Arthritis 134

12 Your Child's Future 137
A Time of Transition 137
The College Route 140

13 Financial Issues 149
Personal Medical Insurance 149
Tips for Helping Meet Medical Expenses 151
Federal Programs 151
State Programs 152

14 Knowing and Protecting Your Child's Rights 155
Your Child's Rights 156
Power in Numbers: Advocating Together 158

IN CONCLUSION 161
APPENDICES 162
Varni/Thompson Pediatric Pain Questionnaire . 162
Body Outline for Pain 164
Classification of Rheumatic Diseases
in Childhood 166

GLOSSARY 170
RESOURCES 179
BIBLIOGRAPHY 184
INDEX 185

ACKNOWLEDGMENTS

Special thanks for content development to

Janet Austin, PhD
Vice President, American Juvenile
  Arthritis Organization and
  Arthritis-Related Groups
Arthritis Foundation

Doyt L. Conn, MD
Senior Vice President,
  Medical Affairs
Arthritis Foundation

Reviewers

Teresa Brady, PhD
Arthritis health professional

Carol Henderson, MS, RD, LD
Dietitian

Susan Klepper, PhD, PT
Physical therapist

Ann Kunkel, BS
Arthritis health professional and
  parent of a child with juvenile
  arthritis

Amye Leong
Diversity specialist and
  motivational speaker

Carol Lindsley, MD
Pediatric rheumatologist

Mary Long, RN
Public policy and advocacy specialist

Paula Nelson, PT
Physical therapist

Holly Nuckols, RN
Nurse

Michael Rapoff, PhD
Behaviorial scientist

Patty Rettig, MSN
Pediatric rheumatology nurse

Barbara Warady, MS, RD, LD
Dietitian

Amy Wenz, OTR/L
Occupational therapist

Larry Zemel, MD
Pediatric rheumatologist

Publishing team

Beth Axtell
Cynthia Bertelsen
Kathryn Born
Elizabeth Compton
Audrey Graham
Adrienne Greer
Milly Hough
Cynthia Kahn
Cindy McDaniel
Bill Otto
Susan Percy
Jennifer Rogers
Dianne Witter

Introduction

Juvenile arthritis. After you've heard the diagnosis, you, your child and family members may feel that your lives will never again be the same. Granted, the extra concerns that go along with having a child with arthritis may at first feel overwhelming, but you'll soon learn that life goes on, despite arthritis. It isn't easy, but with enough knowledge and experience, you will learn the skills necessary to help your child maintain a good quality of life and progress physically, socially and emotionally.

This book suggests practical ways to help make life with arthritis easier. It offers specific tips for day-to-day living, as well as points to keep in mind as you raise your child. *Raising a Child With Arthritis* includes information for parents of toddlers, children, teenagers and young adults. It should be used along with other materials provided by your child's doctors, nurses, social workers and therapists. This book is not meant to take the place of the treatment, advice and guidance provided by your child's health-care team.

As you are reading this book, some words may be unfamiliar or new to you. The glossary (located after the Appendices of this book) provides definitions for some of these terms.

Juvenile arthritis affects girls more commonly than boys. For this reason only, the pronoun "she" or "her" will be used in this book. However, both girls and boys are affected by this group of diseases.

part one
JUVENILE ARTHRITIS: A PRIMER

Approximately 285,000 children in the United States have some form of juvenile arthritis. Arthritis also can be a feature of more than 100 other diseases such as the spondyloarthropathies (ankylosing spondylitis, inflammatory bowel disease, and Reiter's syndrome), and connective tissue diseases (systemic lupus erythematosus, juvenile dermatomyositis, scleroderma, mixed connective tissue disease and vasculitis). Children are also affected by noninflammatory disorders such as fibromyalgia. For convenience, in this book the term juvenile arthritis will be used to refer to arthritis and other musculoskeletal conditions that occur in children.

1

What Is Juvenile Arthritis?

The word arthritis refers to inflammation (swelling, heat and pain) involving the joints. Arthritis is frequently a chronic illness lasting for months or years. When arthritis occurs by age 15 years or younger, it is called juvenile arthritis. There are many different types of arthritis, and there are also a number of related musculoskeletal conditions that are not technically arthritis but that have similar symptoms and treatment. For convenience, in this book the term juvenile arthritis will be used to refer to arthritis and other musculoskeletal conditions that occur in children.

Approximately 285,000 children in the United States have some form of juvenile arthritis. Arthritis can be a feature of more than 100 other diseases such as the spondyloarthropathies (ankylosing spondylitis, inflammatory bowel disease, and Reiter's syndrome), and connective tissue diseases (systemic lupus erythematosus, juvenile dermatomyositis, scleroderma, mixed connective tissue disease and vasculitis). Children are also affected by noninflammatory disorders such as fibromyalgia.

Chronic arthritis in children can involve organs other than the joints. Treatment may involve medications, rehabilitative therapies (physical and occupational therapy) and sometimes surgery. The focus for care is the child and the family. Different health-care specialists may be required at different times during the child's illness. These may include a pediatrician or family practitioner, pediatric rheumatologist, nurse clinician, physical therapist, occupational therapist, dietitian, ophthalmologist, psychologist, nephrologist, neurologist, gastroenterologist, cardiologist, pulmonologist, orthopaedic surgeon, dentist, or social worker. Early diagnosis and appropriate treatment make it possible to manage the disease successfully and reduce possible disability.

Arthritis education is very important for both the child and the family. Helping children and their families cope with a chronic, often unpredictable and frequently painful illness of uncertain outcome presents a great challenge. The American Juvenile Arthritis Organization (AJAO) provides families with networking and educational opportunities through participation in regional and national juvenile arthritis family conferences. Education of school teachers and school administrators is important to ensure the child's educational needs are met. (See page 123 for school issues.)

Diagnosis of Juvenile Arthritis

There is no single test that makes the diagnosis of juvenile arthritis; in fact, it can be difficult to diagnose and treat. The severity of the condition varies widely among individual children and disease type. Your child's medical history, physical findings and selected laboratory tests factor into the physician's diagnosis. Symptoms experienced in the first six months of illness are keys to the diagnosis. The main components of a diagnosis include:

- A comprehensive health history to help determine the length of time symptoms have been present, to rule out other possible causes such as viral infections, and to discover familial patterns that may exist.

- A physical examination to identify joint inflammation (heat, swelling and pain), rashes, nodules and eye problems that may suggest the presence of juvenile arthritis.

- Laboratory tests to help exclude other diseases. These tests may include erythrocyte sedimentation ("sed") rate; antinuclear antibody test (ANA); rheumatoid factor test (RF); hemoglobin; urinalysis (UA) and others.

- X-ray examinations of joints to identify other possible conditions such as infections, tumors or fractures and, later on, to help assess damage to joints due to arthritis.

- Tests of fluids from joints and tissues to check for infections or inflammation.

Types of Juvenile Arthritis and Related Conditions

Juvenile Rheumatoid Arthritis (JRA)

This is the most prevalent form of arthritis in children. The most common features include joint inflammation, muscle and soft tissue tightening or contracture, bone erosion, joint misalignment and altered growth patterns. There are three major types of JRA:

- Polyarticular JRA, which affects five or more joints;
- Pauciarticular JRA, which affects four or fewer joints;
- Systemic JRA, which affects both the joints and the internal organs.

The signs and symptoms of JRA vary from child to child. The specific diagnosis is determined by the presence of active arthritis in one or more joints, lasting for at least six weeks, and the exclusion of other causes of arthritis. Your child's physician may refer your child to a pediatric rheumatologist, a physician who specializes in the treatment of children with arthritis.

In spite of new insights into the cause and considerable advances in treatment, JRA remains a prevalent cause of chronic pain and disability in childhood.

The most common features of JRA are:

- Joint inflammation that causes heat, pain and swelling in the synovium or the lining of the joint. This can cause range-of-motion limitations, joint tenderness when touched, pain during joint movement or increased heat over the joint.

• Tightening and shortening of tendons, ligaments and muscles that cause joint contracture.

• Joint damage caused by long-lasting inflammation that erodes bone and cartilage.

• Altered growth resulting from joint inflammation that either speeds up or slows down the growth centers in bones, causing affected bones to become longer, shorter or bigger than normal.

• Flares of disease activity that can affect joints and internal organs, causing pain, mobility restrictions, fever and fatigue.

The Three Types of JRA

Polyarticular JRA. Polyarticular means "many joints." In this form of arthritis, five or more joints are involved. Girls are affected by polyarticular JRA more frequently than boys. The onset of polyarticular JRA in teenage girls often resembles that of adult rheumatoid arthritis (RA).

Polyarticular JRA:

• Usually affects the small joints of the fingers and hands;

• Usually affects the same joint on both sides of the body;

• Can also affect weight-bearing joints and other joints, especially the knees, hips, ankles, feet, neck and jaw.

Other possible features of polyarticular JRA include:

• Low-grade fever;

• A positive blood test for rheumatoid factor;

• Rheumatoid nodules, or bumps, on an elbow or other points of pressure, from chairs, shoes or other objects.

Pauciarticular JRA. Pauciarticular means "few joints." In this form of JRA, four or fewer joints are affected.

Pauciarticular JRA:

- Usually affects the large joints (knees, ankles or elbows);

- Often affects a particular joint on only one side of the body;

- May cause iridocyclitis, an eye inflammation. This is most frequent in young girls with positive ANA, but may occur at any age, with or without active joint symptoms. (See page 92 for more information about eye care.)

Systemic JRA. This form of JRA affects the body generally with fever and can affect the child's internal organs as well as joints and skin. Boys and girls are equally likely to have systemic JRA, although it is the least common form of JRA. For some children, the systemic symptoms of the disease and the fever go away completely, although the joint-related symptoms of arthritis may remain.

Common features of systemic JRA include:

- High spiking fevers (103 degrees or higher) lasting for weeks or even months;

- A rash consisting of pale red spots that may appear on the child's chest, thighs and sometimes other parts of the body (the rash usually accompanies the fever and may come and go);

- Joint inflammation that accompanies the fever or starts weeks or months later;

- Joint problems that continue long term.

Other possible features include:

- Inflammation of the outer lining of the heart, the heart itself or the lungs;

- Anemia (low red blood count);

- Enlarged lymph nodes, liver or spleen.

Juvenile Spondyloarthropathy Syndromes

These syndromes include juvenile ankylosing spondylitis, seronegative enthesopathy and arthropathy syndrome (SEA syndrome), arthritis associated with inflammatory bowel disease, psoriasis, and Reiter's syndrome. Spondyloarthropathies occur more often in boys than in girls.

Juvenile ankylosing spondylitis generally causes large joint arthritis of the lower extremities, commonly affecting the hips. Frequently an HLA-B27 blood test will be positive, and the rheumatoid factor blood test will be negative.

Reiter's syndrome usually develops as a reactive arthritis after *Shigella*, *Salmonella* or *Yersinia*-associated diarrhea. Onset can be acute with fever and involve many joints. There is a potential for long-term disability from Reiter's syndrome.

Juvenile Psoriatic Arthritis

Psoriatic arthritis symptoms in children include nail pitting or ridging and an atypical rash behind the ears, on the eyelids, elbows, knees and at the scalp line or the navel. A family history of psoriatic arthritis may be present. The joints involved are similar to those involved in juvenile ankylosing spondylitis.

Juvenile Systemic Lupus Erythematosus (SLE, Lupus)

This rarely occurs in children under the age of five; in fact, most children with SLE develop the disease during adolescence. Signs and symptoms are similar to those in adults. Lupus is an episodic disease with a history of symptoms that come and go. This multisystem disease involves symptoms of small blood vessel vasculitis affecting more than one organ system (skin, kidneys, lungs, heart, brain, joints, bone marrow, and/or eyes).

The diagnosis of SLE is made when a combination of several of the following criteria are present:

- Malar rash
- Discoid lupus (affects only the skin)
- Photosensitivity
- Oral or nasal ulcers
- Arthritis

- Inflammation of the heart or lungs
- Neurologic symptoms (psychosis or seizures)
- Kidney involvement
- Anemia, leukopenia, lymphopenia or thrombocytopenia
- Blood tests that show the presence of antinuclear antibodies (ANA) and other specific autoantibodies

Many children with lupus have some form of kidney disease. Central nervous system involvement and cognitive disturbance may be subtle. Pleurisy-like chest pain is one of the most common symptoms among children who have pulmonary (lung) symptoms. Arthritis and arthralgia (joint and muscle pain) are frequent; however, they rarely cause long-term problems.

Sun protection may be important for children with lupus. Your child's physician may recommend sunblock or clothing to provide protection so your child can participate in outdoor daytime activities.

Neonatal lupus syndrome occurs when a newborn of a mother with clinical or serologic evidence of SLE, rheumatoid arthritis (RA), mixed connective tissue disease (MCTD) or Sjögrens syndrome has:

- Congenital complete heart block;
- Low platelet count (thrombocytopenia);
- Rash (erythema annulare);
- Hepatitis.

Juvenile Dermatomyositis (JDMS)

This is an inflammatory disease of unknown cause that affects the skin and muscle. About 20 percent of children with JDMS have arthritis.

The condition is characterized by muscle inflammation and may be accompanied by vasculitis (inflammation of small blood vessels) in the skin, muscle and gastrointestinal tract. Diagnosis requires the presence of a typical rash, as well as at least three of the following criteria:

- Elevated muscle enzymes;
- Muscle weakness in the same muscles on both sides of the body;
- Evidence of vasculitis or chronic inflammation on muscle biopsy;
- An electromyogram that confirms inflammatory myopathy (inflamed muscles).

Juvenile dermatomyositis occurs most often in children between the ages of 5 and 14 years and is more common in girls. The muscle weakness children with JDMS experience causes difficulty running, climbing stairs or getting up from a sitting position on the floor. Muscle pain is not a frequent complaint. Gastrointestinal involvement can lead to poor absorption of medications, ulceration and perforation of the bowel.

Juvenile Vasculitis

Vasculitis can be both a primary childhood disease and a feature of other syndromes, including dermatomyositis (JDMS) and systemic lupus erythematosus (SLE).

One of the most common forms of vasculitis in children is Henoch-Schönlein purpura (HSP). This syndrome consists of a rash, arthritis, abdominal pain and renal dysfunction. Signs and symptoms may occur for several days or weeks. The rash progresses from red to purple to brown and most commonly is located on the lower extremities.

Polyarteritis nodosa is a vasculitis of small and medium-sized blood vessels. Symptoms are similar to those that adults experience. It can affect any organ system of the body, but most frequently involves the skin, peripheral nerves, kidneys, intestinal tract and joints.

Kawasaki disease symptoms typically include fever, rash on the palms and soles, swollen lips that crack and bleed, and swollen lymph nodes. Heart involvement is the most serious complication of this form of vasculitis, which occurs in very young children (boys more often than girls).

Some other forms of juvenile vasculitis include cutaneous polyarteritis, Wegener's granulomatosis, Takayasu's arteritis and Behçet's syndrome.

Juvenile Sclerodermas

Juvenile scleroderma is rare but includes both localized and systemic disease. The skin, muscles, tendons, joints and bones are affected, often significantly interfering with growth.

Localized scleroderma includes several types of skin lesions:

- Morphea is a type of skin lesion that has at least one plaque of thickened skin, excluding post-traumatic skin scarring;

- Linear scleroderma has at least one band-like tight lesion involving skin and subcutaneous tissues.

Systemic scleroderma is similar to that experienced by adults and includes Raynaud's phenomenon as well as skin, musculoskeletal, gastrointestinal, lung, heart or kidney involvement.
 Systemic scleroderma can be in one of two forms:

- CREST Syndrome – the name is an acronym formed by the first letters of key characteristics; it involves calcinosis of the skin, Raynaud's phenomenon, esophageal dysmotility, sclerodactyly and telangiectasia of the skin and mucus membranes.

- Systemic Sclerosis is characterized by generalized diffuse skin thickening or loss of skin elasticity and often includes involvement of the lung, kidneys or heart.

Mixed Connective Tissue Disease (MCTD)
This condition is uncommon, but may include features of arthritis, scleroderma, dermatomyositis (JDMS), and lupus (SLE) at some time during the illness. It is characterized by the presence of specific autoantibodies to nuclear proteins.

Overlap Syndromes
Children may have other overlapping diseases with features of chronic arthritis, scleroderma, dermatomyositis (JDMS), lupus (SLE) and Sjögren's syndrome.

Other Connective Tissue Related Diagnoses
Raynaud's Phenomenon. This syndrome involves sudden, reversible "dead-white" or bluish discoloration of the extremities (most commonly the fingers) caused by exposure to cold and occurring in the absence of another recognized connective tissue disease. Raynaud's phenomenon is often a symptom of connective tissue diseases, especially scleroderma.

Primary Sjögren's Syndrome. Symptoms of dry eyes, dry mouth and swelling of glands near the ear, in the absence of another defined connective tissue disease may signal primary Sjögren's syndrome. Sjögren's syndrome is often called sicca syndrome if it is a symptom of connective tissue diseases.

Panniculitis. This may be recognized by generalized painful nodules beneath the skin. Diagnosis is made by skin biopsy with evidence of inflammatory cells in the subcutaneous tissue.

Erythema Nodosum. Painful, erythematous nodules over the upper surfaces of the legs and sometimes the arms are the primary symtom of this disease.

Juvenile Noninflammatory Disorders

Benign Hypermobility Syndromes
Generalized hypermobility of the joints is associated with musculoskeletal pain but not with underlying connective tissue disease. Hypermobility syndrome represents extreme variation of the normal range of joint motion. Girls are more often affected than boys, and frequently there is a family history of hypermobility.

Pain Syndromes
Noninflammatory disorders are important causes of chronic or recurrent pain in children. They arise from a variety of causes – some possibly as the result of injury and others of unknown cause.

Growing Pains. The cause of growing pains is unknown. They occur equally among boys and girls. They cause deep aching, bilateral cramping pains in the thigh or calf experienced usually in the evening or during the night; the pain typically responds to massage and analgesia. Physical and laboratory exams are normal.

Primary Fibromyalgia Syndrome. Fibromyalgia is characterized by widespread, often ill-defined musculoskeletal aching and stiffness. The child may have constant fatigue, disturbed sleep patterns, anxiety and depression. Diagnosis is based on history and demonstration of multiple tender points (at least three) at certain characteristic locations on the body. Arthritis does not occur and the child may appear otherwise healthy. The pain is very real but is not caused by a serious underlying disease. Treatment consists of a combination of exercise, relaxation and medication.

Reflex Sympathetic Dystrophy. Children and adolescents with reflex sympathetic dystrophy (RSD) have a history of constant pain and increasing disability in the distal, or farthest, part of an extremity that is exacerbated by even mild activity. The involved extremity may have diffuse swelling, tenderness, coolness, and mottling or blotching of the skin. Even a light touch may cause severe discomfort, and attempts to move the limb are extremely painful. Treatment includes pain control to allow physical therapy of the affected limb.

Overuse Syndromes

Syndromes related to overuse of joints occur with considerable frequency in children and adolescents. The growing child is particularly susceptible to overuse injuries.

Summary

As you can see, there are many different forms of arthritis in children, and diagnosis can be difficult. The goal of this book is to help you learn as much as possible about your child's condition so you can be an active member of your child's health-care team and an advocate for her in seeking treatment. With early diagnosis and proper management, it is possible to manage juvenile arthritis successfully and reduce potential disability.

Your Child's Health-Care Team

Your child's medical care should be a team effort. The team includes you, your child and your child's doctor (a pediatrician or a pediatric rheumatologist), and may also include a nurse, physical therapist, occupational therapist, pharmacist, nutritionist and mental health or social worker. Other health professionals may be a part of the team, depending on your child's special needs.

To make sure your child gets the best care possible, it's important to inform all members of the team about her condition and treatment. Also remember that the more involved she is in the decision-making and treatment discussions, the more likely she will be to comply with her treatment program. Urge her health-care team members to talk directly to her, rather than exclusively with you, whenever possible.

Here are a few tips to help you and your child communicate with team members:

- Prepare for each visit. Write down your questions and a few sentences about how your child is doing. Include a complete list of the medications your child takes and the dosages. This could be called a progress report. Remember that you often have weeks prior to the appointment but only a brief time with your medical team members. If your child is old enough, she should prepare her own questions and progress report. Keep in mind that the firsthand information you and your child provide the team members is valuable. They rely on both of you to be as specific as possible when reporting information.

- Learn from each visit. Always ask for explanations if you don't understand. Repeat questions if you need more explanation. Health professionals really do know how important it is for you to understand, and teaching is part of their job. During your visit or after you get home, write down notes from the visit to help you recall important information later on. You might try keeping a journal of all key information about your child. After all, the more you and your child know, the better "partners" you and your health-care team will become.

- Keep all team members informed. You and your child are the central players in your health-care team, and are in the best position to make sure all team members know about your total treatment plan, medications and progress. The stronger the partnerships with you, your child and her health-care team members, the better the results will be.

How to Get the Most from Your Child's Medical Visits

Because you'll probably have to see your child's doctor and other members of her health-care team often, it is to her benefit to make the best use of your time together. Following are several things to keep in mind before, during and after your visits.

Before Your Child's Visit

The first step in creating a good partnership with your child's health-care team is to find a doctor you and your child like. Chronic disease treatment generally involves a long-term doctor-patient relationship, so it's important that you find someone you feel is competent and has the qualities you and your child consider important.

To help narrow your search, contact your local Arthritis Foundation chapter and request a copy of their arthritis specialists referral list, which will include adult and pediatric rheumatologists.

Following are some other steps to take before your visit:

- Call ahead for an appointment, preferably when no emergency exists.

- Arrange to have your child's medical records transferred to the doctor's office if she is a new patient.

- Consider having routine blood tests or other diagnostic tests done before your child's appointment if she is already a patient. This way, her doctor can discuss the results with you during your visit.

- If it will make you or your child feel more comfortable, arrange to have an adult friend or relative accompany you to the appointment so you'll have another set of ears to process the information.

- Write down everything you want to ask or tell your child's doctor. With your child's input, prepare a brief progress report. Her doctor might ask her: Have you been following your treatment plan? How have you been feeling? Have you had any problems? What has been happening in your life? Discuss these questions with your child ahead of time, and jot down the answers. If your child has pain, ask her to describe how bad it is on a scale of zero to 10, with 10 being the worst. Ask her to make a comparison, such as "a numbing kind of pain, like a toothache" or "a stabbing pain."

- Know the names and the dosages of all medicines your child is taking, including prescription and over-the-counter medications. If she is taking several medications, bring her pill bottles, especially if she has medications prescribed by more than one doctor. If this is a return visit, list any medication refills she needs. Be prepared to discuss any medicines that are not helping or are causing side effects.

During the Visit

Tell your doctor why you and your child are there. If this is your child's first visit, communicate her personal medical history. This is important, especially since she may be treated by several health-care professionals.

Be selective when discussing your concerns and bring up the most important ones first, because your time with the doctor will be limited. Concentrate on the symptoms that bother your child the most and on the major questions you have. Encourage your child to answer the doctor's questions herself when possible and to be specific in reporting her progress. If she hasn't been feeling well, or if you are not happy with her treatment, tell the doctor.

Also tell the doctor if pain or stiffness prevents your child from doing certain activities that are important to her, such as participating in school sports or riding her bicycle. If she is having such difficulties, other members of her health-care team, such as a physical therapist, an occupational therapist, a psychologist or a social worker, can work with her to help improve her ability to function.

Take notes on the doctor's comments, and especially on any changes in the treatment program or medication. An alternative is to tape record the visit. The recording can be a helpful source of information once you return home. Make sure you and your child understand what to expect from a treatment and how long it will take to work. If the doctor changes your child's treatment program, make sure you understand why and what to expect. In the long run, your child will make the most progress if you carefully follow the treatment plan.

Remind the doctor about your child's interests and needs. Remembering her interests and needs helps the doctor develop the best program for her treatment. For example, the doctor may be able to help your child keep pain in her knee under control so that she can continue to play baseball. Or if your child's daily activities make it difficult for her to take medication four times a day, her doctor may be able to prescribe a medication taken only twice a day.

Always ask the doctor to explain anything about your child's arthritis or treatment program that you don't understand. Try repeating what you think you heard. If the doctor's instructions still aren't clear to you, ask for written patient education materials and an explanation from the nurse before leaving the office.

Tell the doctor about any concerns you or your child have about her treatment. Don't be afraid to request information on treatment options or to suggest a change in your child's treatment. Managing her arthritis and controlling pain and joint damage are ongoing processes that have to be monitored continually. The doctor relies on your child's feedback to determine how well parts of the treatment program are working. The doctor may need to change some aspect of the treatment if:

- The treatment isn't working;
- Your child is experiencing too many side effects; or
- The treatment is too inconvenient.

Ask the doctor about preventive measures to help relieve discomfort, minimize disability and improve your child's health. These may include such lifestyle changes as participating in mild exercises, losing weight, reducing her stress level and pacing activities.

Don't be afraid to ask the doctor how much something will cost or if less expensive options exist. Ask if your child can take generic or non-brand-name medications, which are usually less expensive. Some, but not all, arthritis medications are available in a generic form. Once you've found a medication that works for your child, ask the doctor to prescribe it in larger quantities, which will cost less. You also may be able to get better prices on medications through discount pharmacy services.

Encourage your child to tell the doctor about her accomplishments, especially with the self-management/lifestyle aspects of her treatment program. Those things that have helped her may help others.

SPECIFIC THINGS TO TELL THE DOCTOR

- Where it hurts

- When it hurts

- How long it has hurt

- If you have noticed any swelling

- What daily activities your child used to do easily that are now difficult

- If your child has ever injured the joint in an accident, from overuse at school or from participation in a hobby

- If anyone in your family has had similar problems

- Important events in your child's personal and social life that may affect her arthritis and the way she takes care of herself

- Any unusual symptoms or side effects, such as a skin rash, sores in the mouth, dizziness or stomach problems

SPECIFIC QUESTIONS TO ASK THE DOCTOR

- What type of arthritis does my child have?

- What is happening to her body as a result of her arthritis?

- What is the purpose of this treatment?

- How and when will this treatment make my child feel better?

- Can we expect any negative side effects from this treatment?

- What should we do if my child experiences side effects?

- What type of symptoms require a call or visit to the doctor between appointments?

- What will happen if we leave my child's arthritis untreated?

- What are the treatment options (in terms of medications and/or therapies)?

- Which other health professionals should my child see?

- What classes might help me learn more about my child's arthritis?

- What lifestyle changes should we consider for my child?

- What types of assistive devices can help my child accomplish her daily tasks?

- What school or home accommodations should be made?

- How is my child's arthritis likely to change in the future?

- When should my child return for a follow-up visit?

- Are there any community programs designed for children with arthritis available?

- When should I schedule the next appointment?

After the Visit

If you are not satisfied with some part of your child's diagnosis or treatment, discuss it with the physician and seek a second opinion from another doctor if you feel it is needed. Ask your child's doctor to recommend a consulting physician. Then ask that a copy of your child's medical records be sent to the consulting physician.

Usually the consulting physician will call or write a letter to your child's doctor, stating findings and giving advice for treatment. Discuss the second opinion with your child's own doctor and decide if it should make any difference in the treatment plan.

If your child visits a rheumatologist or other specialist for a second opinion, you need to decide if that doctor will have an ongoing role in your child's care. Some children are treated for certain forms of arthritis by their primary care physician and may never visit a rheumatologist. Other children with more active forms of arthritis are treated by their primary care physician in consultation with a rheumatologist. Some children with severe forms of arthritis see only a rheumatologist.

Make sure your child follows her treatment program. Developing a partnership with your child's health-care team means your child needs to try her best to follow the treatment program. All too often, children fail to follow their health-care providers' instructions for one reason or another. They may forget or get too busy.

Think of your child's treatment program as her commitment to her own health, and encourage her to make it a regular part of her lifestyle as much as possible. For example, place her medication usage chart (see page 102) on her mirror, bathroom door or on the refrigerator to remind her to take her medications. Encourage her to make a habit of doing her exercises at the same time in the same place every day. If your child finds that she cannot follow her treatment program, tell her doctor or other members of her health-care team. They may be able to change her treatment or suggest some alternative treatment.

It's very important not to change your child's treatment program on your own. If your child has a problem with her treatment program, talk to her doctor. Many children stop taking their medicines or stop other parts of their program once they start feeling better. Or, if they don't start to feel better right away, they become discouraged. Others stop their treatment because they don't fully understand how it will help their symptoms. Stopping your child's treatment for any of these reasons can be harmful. Some arthritis medicines and other parts of her treatment program may take considerable time, even months, to work. Often the success of a treatment program depends on following it consistently. Be sure to ask her doctor what symptoms should change so that you know what to expect.

You may read or hear about new treatments for arthritis, but don't follow other medical advice without first checking with your child's own doctor. Some of these may be harmless, but others can be dangerous. If your child has already tried an alternative treatment, be sure to tell her doctor, because it may affect the quality of her current treatment.

Be aware of how your child feels and functions. This means knowing the side effects of her medicines, how she feels after she exercises, and how she is doing in school and social situations. You and your child may find it helpful to record your findings in your diaries or journals and then share this information with the doctor during your child's next appointment.

Being aware of how your child feels also means being aware of how other parts of her treatment program affect her. For example, does her wrist splint feel comfortable? If you aren't sure about part of your child's treatment program, call the doctor. You may also call your local Arthritis Foundation office and ask for information about arthritis medications and treatment.

Summary

Now you have a clearer idea of your and your child's roles in a partnership with her health-care team. You can help them help your child by:

- Taking an active role in your child's medical care;
- Making sure your child follows her treatment program;
- Making the most of office visits;
- Talking honestly with the health-care team.

Remember, the members of your child's health-care team are people, just like you. There is no reason to be in awe of them, nor is there any need to blindly follow orders without asking questions. Their job is to provide your child with good medical care. Remember that together, you and your health-care team are your child's care coordinators.

part two
TREATMENT GOALS AND STRATEGIES

You and your health-care team members have several goals in mind when treating your child's arthritis. Part two of this book will explain many of the strategies used to meet these goals.

Reduce inflammation. *Taking the prescribed medication and avoiding activities that put excessive stress on joints helps reduce inflammation and joint damage.*

Relieve pain. *Taking medication as prescribed, using heat or cold treatments, practicing relaxation and performing prescribed exercises will help ease pain.*

Stay active. *Appropriate exercises and play activities can help prevent stiffness and loss of motion. They also can help maintain the ability to perform daily tasks and enhance self-esteem.*

Prevent joint destruction. *By protecting painful joints and by wearing lightweight splints when prescribed, your child may be able to slow down or prevent joint destruction.*

Understand the disease. *Learning more about what arthritis is, what kind of treatment to expect and how to communicate and be responsible for her activities will make it easier for your child to cope with the problems arthritis causes.*

Participate in regular childhood activities. *Attending school, making friends, having special interests and hobbies, and doing the usual things other children her age do will help her build self-esteem and become a responsible, mature adult.*

Your child's treatment program will depend on her type of arthritis and the specific symptoms. The treatment plan generally includes a combination of medications, exercise, eye care, dental care and good nutrition. Surgery may be necessary, but that is rare. Although there is no cure for most types of arthritis, medications for children are designed to reduce swelling, pain, heat and tenderness of joints, thereby improving joint motion. Some medicines are used to reduce inflammation in other organs such as the eyes, kidneys and heart.

Medications

The proper use of medication is one of the keys to managing childhood arthritis. Keep in mind that as the course of the disease changes, as your child gets older, gains weight or has side effects, the dosage or the medicine itself may change. Taking the medications on the prescribed schedule will help provide maximum relief of stiffness and pain and prevent or limit joint damage.

Your child's medication may include a combination of different drugs. Many children with arthritis take more than one medication. Arthritis varies a good deal from child to child; therefore the treatment must be individualized for each person. Changes may occur from time to time as your child's condition changes and/or new medications become available. For these reasons, it is not a good idea to compare what is prescribed for your child with the medicine another child takes.

Some medications used to treat juvenile arthritis have Food and Drug Administration (FDA) approval specifically for use in children; others are approved for the general public but not specifically for children. That is because, until recently, children were not routinely included in FDA trials of new medications. It is up to your doctor's discretion to prescribe medications that are generally accepted by the medical community as being helpful for children.

The immediate goal of drug therapy is to reduce inflammation, relieve pain and swelling and maximize function. Long range goals are to alter the progress of the disease and to prevent the destruction of bone, cartilage and soft tissues such as tendons and joint capsules.

Nonsteroidal Anti-Inflammatory Drugs (NSAIDs)

This group of medications is used in most types of juvenile arthritis to help control pain and inflammation. NSAIDs must be taken for at least four weeks before benefits become apparent. Children should receive appropriate laboratory evaluations to monitor medication toxicity. Commonly used NSAIDs include:

- ibuprofen (*Motrin, Advil, Motrin IB, Nuprin*)
- naproxen (*Naprosyn*)
- tolmetin sodium (*Tolectin*)
- ketoprofen (*Orudis, Oruvail, Actron, Orudis KT*)
- flurbiprofen (*Ansaid*)
- fenoprofen calcium (*Nalfon*)
- sulindac (*Clinoril*)
- meclofenamate sodium (*Meclomen*)
- diclofenac sodium (*Voltaren*)
- piroxicam (*Feldene*)
- oxaprozin (*Daypro*)
- nabumetone (*Relafen*)
- indomethacin (*Indocin*)
- etodolac (*Lodine*)
- ketorolac (*Toradol*)

These medications come in liquid or pill form and are taken from one to four times per day, depending on the individual drug. Possible side effects include stomach pain, nausea and vomiting; anemia; headache; severe abdominal pain and peptic ulcer; fragility and scarring of the skin (especially with naproxen); and difficulty concentrating in school.

Salicylates

Aspirin is another non-inflammatory medication that is used to control joint pain and swelling and to reduce fever. It is typically given three or four times a day. This category includes aspirin (acetylated salicylates) such as *Anacin, Ascriptin, Bayer, Bufferin, Ecotrin* and *Excedrin,* and the nonacetylated salicylates, *Disalcid* and *Trilisate.*

Possible side effects include stomach pains; stomach bleeding; black, tarry stools; and reactions to high levels of salicylates in the blood (rapid or deep breathing, ringing in the ears, decrease in hearing, drowsiness, nausea, vomiting, irritability and unusual behavior). Gastrointestinal side effects are less common and less severe with non-acetylated salicylates. Reye's syndrome is a rare condition that sometimes occurs in children who have chicken pox or the flu and who are taking aspirin. Symptoms include frequent vomiting, very painful headaches, unusual behavior, extreme tiredness and disorientation.

Disease-Modifying Antirheumatic Drugs (DMARDs)

These medications do not produce immediate pain relief or anti-inflammatory effect, but induce beneficial effects that modify the natural progress of joint disease (cartilage and bone erosion or destruction) weeks to months after therapy is begun. Current wisdom shows that DMARDs should be used early in the course of JRA to reduce joint damage. These drugs are often used in combination with NSAIDs and glucocorticoids. DMARDs all have potential side effects, but the benefits outweigh them in most cases. Problems can be detected through frequent and diligent monitoring. These medications include hydroxy-chloroquine, penicillamine, sulfasalazine, gold compounds, methotrexate, azathioprine, cyclophosphamide and cyclosporine.

Hydroxychloroquine sulfate (*Plaquenil*): This drug is usually given in pill form. Side effects include upset stomach, skin rash and eye damage (a child taking this drug should have her eyes examined at least every six months by an ophthalmologist).

Sulfasalazine *(Azulfidine)*: This drug is usually given in pill form. Side effects may include stomach upset, aches, diarrhea, dizziness, headache, light sensitivity, itching, appetite loss, liver abnormalities, lowered blood count, nausea, vomiting and rash.

Gold compounds (oral gold compound auranofin [*Ridaura*] and injectable gold compounds *Myochrysine* and *Solganol*): The oral form is taken daily. Injections are usually given every week for five or six months, then once or twice a month for as long as necessary. Side effects may include skin rash, mouth sores, kidney problems, a low blood count and anemia. Diarrhea is a complication of the oral form of gold compound.

Methotrexate *(Rheumatrex)*: Given by pill or injection in weekly doses, the injectable form can be taken orally. Regular laboratory monitoring is important. Side effects may include nausea, mouth sores, diarrhea, low white blood cell count, lung irritation and liver abnormalities (although no children should be drinking alcohol, it is especially important for those taking methotrexate). There is a risk of birth defects if methotrexate is taken during pregnancy. A folic acid supplement will likely be prescribed to reduce side effects.

Azathioprine *(Imuran)*: This drug is given in pill form. Side effects include fever and chills, loss of appetite, nausea or vomiting, skin rash, unusual bleeding or bruising, unusual tiredness or weakness, and, rarely, sterility.

Cyclosporine *(Sandimmune)*: Given in liquid or pill form, this drug's side effects include bleeding, tender or enlarged gums, fluid retention, high blood pressure, increase in hair growth, kidney problems, loss of appetite, trembling or shaking of hands and tremors.

Glucocorticoid Drugs

Also known as corticosteroids, glucocorticoid drugs include cortisone, dexamethasone, hydrocortisone, methylprednisolone, prelone and prednisone. These drugs are the most potent anti-inflammatory agents used in the treatment of rheumatic diseases. Because of their side effects, they must be used with caution. If glucocorticoid drugs are prescribed, the lowest possible dose should be used for the shortest length of time. Usually the drug is given by mouth as a pill or liquid *(Pediapred)*. It can also be given as an injection into the joint itself or into a muscle or vein.

Possible side effects include high blood pressure, osteoporosis (thinning of the bones), Cushing's syndrome (weight gain, moonface, thin skin, muscle weakness, and brittle bones), cataracts, slowing of the child's growth rate, reduced resistance to infection, mood swings, increased appetite and weight gain, and increased risk for ulcers. The side effects are dose-related and can be reduced by using the lowest dose that will control the symptoms. Additional calcium and vitamin D may reduce glucocorticoid's effects on bones.

Corticosteroid eye drops are sometimes used to treat eye inflammation, and corticosteroid creams may be prescribed for inflammation of the skin.

Analgesics

Analgesics like acetaminophen and tramadol do not relieve inflammation, but they do provide pain relief. They should be taken with other medications only under a physician's advice. Side effects of tramadol *(Ultram)* include dizziness, nausea, constipation, headache and sleepiness.

Biologic Therapies

Intravenous immunoglobulin (IVIG) is used to treat a number of childhood rheumatic diseases, but primarily for vasculitis, polymyositis and dermatomyositis. It is given intravenously usually once a month. Side effects include risk of anaphylaxis (allergic reaction). Researchers currently are developing other forms of experimental biologic therapies.

Medication Guidelines

For your child to get the full benefit from her medications, you need to understand the way all medications, including arthritis medications, are prescribed by your doctor. Ask your child's doctor or nurse for instructions in writing, and keep asking questions until you understand. Explain the information to your child in words she can understand and encourage her to ask questions, too.

QUESTIONS TO ASK ABOUT EACH MEDICATION

- What is its name?

- Why is it prescribed?

- How much should be taken, and when?

- How can I tell if it's working?

- What are the possible side effects?

- What should I do if any side effects occur?

- What should I do if my child vomits soon after taking the medication?

- What should I do if my child misses a dose?

- Are there any special guidelines, such as taking the medication with meals?

- Is there a handout that describes the medication and its side effects?

Keep in mind the following medication guidelines:

- Make certain your child takes the medication on schedule and with or without food as directed. Explain the schedule to her teacher or school nurse so that your child will be able to take her medication on schedule in school, too. (See page 123 on school issues.)

- Do not make any changes in dosage unless you check with the doctor.

- Be alert to the possibility of medication interactions. When two or more drugs act in combination, unwanted side effects may occur. These effects can be unpleasant or even dangerous.

- If you suspect your child is not taking medication properly, talk with her about it. Remind her why her medication is important. You should also discuss this with her doctor at the next visit. Sometimes urging the team members to talk directly to your child (instead of to you) will help her feel more in charge. This can make her more willing to comply. Further suggestions for helping your child take her medications regularly can be found in the chapter "Following the Medical Treatment Program" on page 97.

- If your child is having trouble swallowing pills, have her practice by letting a small piece of sugarless hard candy or an ice chip melt in her mouth until it is about the size of a pill, and then swallowing it. You can also give her a straw to use to direct a stream of water toward the back of her throat to make the pill easier to swallow.

- Keep the medication in clearly marked containers, out of the reach of younger children. Check the supply frequently to make sure you refill the prescription in time. Keeping track of the supply also helps you to know if the correct number of pills is being taken.

- If your child develops a cold, flu, chicken pox, or other childhood disease, consult her doctor. It may be necessary to temporarily stop the arthritis medication while your child is ill.

Saving Money on Medicines

Medications usually cost less if they can be bought in quantity. Once you know that your child will be taking a certain medication regularly, ask the doctor to prescribe it in larger quantities; also ask if it is available as a generic. Ask the pharmacist how long the medication will keep, how to store it properly, and how to check it for freshness. Be sure to check the label on the medicine bottle for the expiration date.

You can save money if you shop for the best prices. Phone several pharmacies to check on price information. You will find that prices vary from store to store. Many prescription plans will mail order a 90-day supply at a reduced cost.

Summary

There are a variety of medications used to treat children with arthritis. Medications are prescribed with the goal of relieving pain, reducing inflammation and maximizing function. Long-range goals are to slow or stop the progress of the disease and prevent joint damage. Many arthritis medications must be taken regularly to be effective. Learning all you can about your child's medications and how they should be taken will ensure your child gets the most benefit possible from them.

Physical Activity

Exercise is one of the basics of treatment for childhood arthritis. Make sure that your child has an exercise program designed just for her by a physiatrist, occupational therapist or a physical therapist who is familiar with juvenile arthritis. An exercise program for your child will help to keep or regain joint motion; relieve stiffness in joints; prevent joint misalignment; prevent, lessen or correct muscle weakness; maintain flexibility; and keep as high a level of function and physical fitness as possible for everyday activities.

Exercise

Why Daily Exercise Is Important
The pain and swelling of childhood arthritis can make it hard for your child to move her affected joints. Loss of mobility can result if a joint is not moved through its range of motion for a period of time. Range of motion refers to the distance a joint can be moved in all directions. If a joint is not often moved in this manner, the muscles and tissue around the joint can become weak and tight, creating a contracture, or frozen

joint that cannot be moved. Thus, a daily exercise program that takes each of your child's affected joints through its complete range of motion will lessen stiffness, loss of motion and misalignment.

Normal motion in joints is necessary for everyday tasks such as walking, dressing and combing hair. If tightness develops in certain joints, it will be hard for your child to do the things that other children her age can do. Regular exercise can help her remain flexible and mobile, making it easier to stay active like other children.

Exercise is healthy for everyone. Why not set a good example by doing your own workout at the same time your child does? Maybe other family members can join in. The United States Surgeon General recommends 30 minutes of moderate physical activity at least four days per week for everyone. You can add music or change the order of your child's routine so it doesn't get boring. Teenagers might enjoy getting together after school or over the weekend to exercise to music. They not only get their exercises done, but can have a fun social experience, too. Exercises can also be done in shorter segments; for example, three 10-minute sessions. If your child is having difficulty exercising regularly, all of these variations can make exercising more fun. Ask the physical therapist for more ideas - he or she will be glad to help.

When to Exercise

Assist your child with her exercises every day at the same time. Your child's exercise program will then become a regular part of her daily routine. Doing the exercises at the same time every day also will help you detect any day-to-day changes in your child's joints.

Exercises should be done on both good and bad days. Vigorous exercise ideally should be done during the time when her affected joints are the least stiff and painful. Gentle exercise can help ease stiffness. It may be more comfortable and easier for your child to do the exercises during or after a warm bath. Heat relaxes stiff joints and helps relieve pain and muscle spasms that restrict joint motion.

Change your child's program and do the exercises less vigorously if she is having a flare (an intense return of pain, inflammation and stiffness). Joints may appear hot, swollen or reddish. Don't force any exercise during a flare. However, make sure that she at least makes an attempt to move each joint within the limit she can tolerate. Keep in mind that skipping exercise can cause affected joints to become stiff or lose some of their range of motion.

Types of Exercise

The major types of exercises for childhood arthritis are range-of-motion, strengthening and endurance exercises.

Active range-of-motion exercises are exercises that your child can do herself to move each joint as far as it will go in all directions. These maintain joint function and help restore joint motion if it has already been lost.

Active assistive range-of-motion exercises (also called passive range-of-motion exercises) are exercises in which someone helps your child move her joints through their ranges of motion. Usually these are done when a child is very young or when a child is having a flare and her joints are quite painful and stiff. These may also be done when a joint is no longer in a flare but has lost motion, requiring assistance to help the child overcome the tightness. Have your child's therapist or physician show you how to perform these exercises with your child.

Strengthening exercises help maintain or increase the strength of muscles. Strong muscles help keep joints stable and more comfortable.

Endurance exercises promote fitness of the heart and blood vessels. They make your child's lungs more efficient and give her more stamina so she doesn't tire as quickly. Swimming is an example of a good endurance exercise for a child with arthritis because it won't damage joints. Endurance exercises that may cause joint damage include some high-impact aerobics programs and running.

Guidelines for Performing Exercises

Your child's therapist will teach you the correct way to do each of the exercises in your child's program. Keep in mind the following tips when your child performs her exercises:

- Always remember that a home exercise program should include a warm-up, a time for exercise and other movement activities, and a cool-down.

• Exercises should be done on a firm but padded surface, such as a floor with a carpet or rug. Don't let your child perform exercises on a bed. It is too soft and doesn't provide enough support.

• Have your child move her own limbs as much as possible while exercising. Using a game such as "Simon says" is a good way to get a young child to move her limbs without help.

• Each exercise should be done slowly and smoothly.

• Your child should move each joint to the point of discomfort, hold that position for about 10 seconds, and then slowly move the joint back to a position that doesn't hurt.

• Repeat each exercise several times, trying to move the joint a little further each time, until the full range of motion is completed.

• If a joint is very inflamed (hot, red or swollen), your child should only do gentle range-of-motion exercises that do not put any weight on the joint.

• If your child resists you when you try to help her, stop for a moment to relax, and try again. Explain to an older child that the exercises will be less painful if she helps you do the motion, rather than resisting the motion.

• Any discomfort your child may have during the range-of-motion exercises should stop after exercising. If discomfort persists for two hours afterwards or if she exhibits signs of inflammation (if the joint is warm or looks more swollen or red), the exercise has been too intense. The next time, see that she does the exercise less vigorously. When a new exercise is added to a program, your child may feel mild soreness the next day. This is normal and often occurs when a muscle is stretched gently. Help your child learn the difference between joint pain after exercise and mild muscle soreness from a new activity.

The exercises shown on the following pages are examples of those often prescribed for children who have arthritis. They are not meant to replace an individual exercise program prescribed by a doctor, physical therapist or occupational therapist.

For example, if your child's knee has become so bent that she cannot fully straighten it, she needs some exercises prescribed just for her to restore it to its normal range of motion.

Before your child attempts these exercises, review them with her doctor and physical therapist. Do these only with their approval.

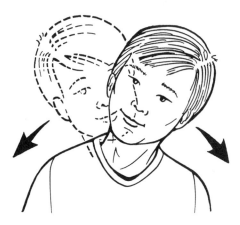

Figure 1. NECK
Tilt the head to each side, with the ear toward the shoulder. Don't lift the shoulder. Repeat 2-3 times on each side.

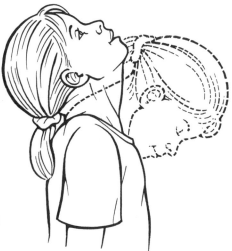

Figure 2. NECK
Tilt the head backward, with the chin up, without moving the body backward. Then bring the head forward. Try to touch the chin to the chest. Repeat 2-3 times. Check with your therapist or physician if you have neck problems.

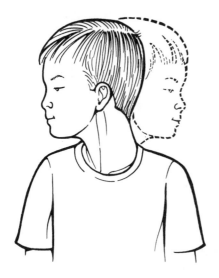

Figure 3. NECK
Turn the head toward one shoulder and then the other. Repeat 2-3 times on each side.

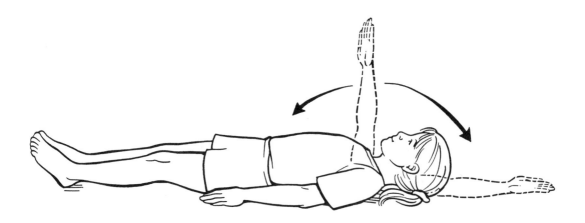

Figure 4. SHOULDER
Lie on the floor with both arms at your sides. Raise one arm over the head, keeping the elbow straight, until the back of the hand reaches the floor. Return the arm slowly to the side. Repeat this exercise with the other arm. Repeat, alternating arms, 2-3 times.

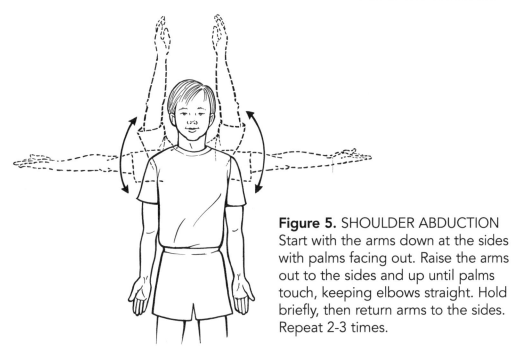

Figure 5. SHOULDER ABDUCTION
Start with the arms down at the sides with palms facing out. Raise the arms out to the sides and up until palms touch, keeping elbows straight. Hold briefly, then return arms to the sides. Repeat 2-3 times.

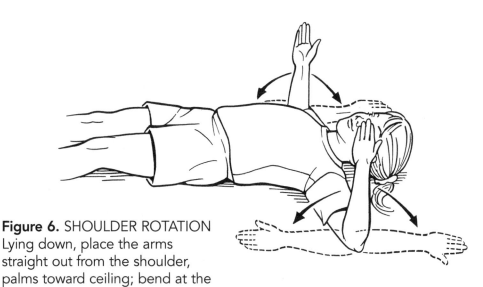

Figure 6. SHOULDER ROTATION
Lying down, place the arms straight out from the shoulder, palms toward ceiling; bend at the elbow with the fingers pointing toward ceiling; roll arms forward so the hands point straight down toward feet (internal rotation); roll arms backward so the hands point toward the head (external rotation). Repeat 2-3 times.

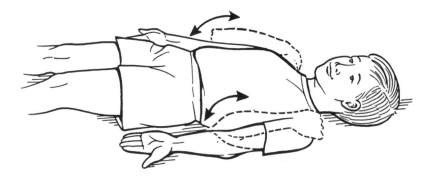

Figure 7. ELBOW
Lie on floor with both arms at sides, palms facing the ceiling. Bring hands to shoulders by bending elbows. Return hands to the floor by straightening elbows.

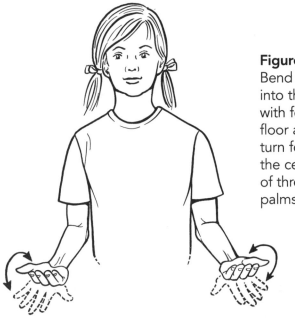

Figure 8. ELBOW
Bend elbows and hold them into the sides of the body, with forearms parallel to the floor and palms down; slowly turn forearms so palms face the ceiling; hold to the count of three and turn arms so palms face the floor again.

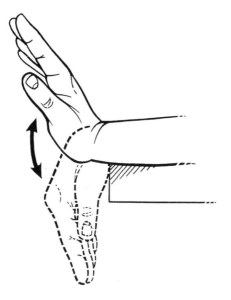

Figure 9. WRIST
With the forearm resting firmly on a table top and the hand hanging over the edge of the table, bend the wrist up as far as possible. Hold. Bend the wrist down as far as possible. Hold. Repeat 2-3 times.

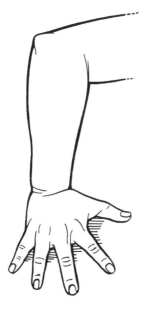

Figure 10. WRIST
Place the hand on a table or other flat surface. Raise elbow toward ceiling until wrinkles appear at the wrist.

Figure 11. WRIST
Grasp the hand with the opposite hand. Put the palms together, with fingers around the opposite hand. Push the hand backward, stretching the wrist. Hold. Repeat 2-3 times.

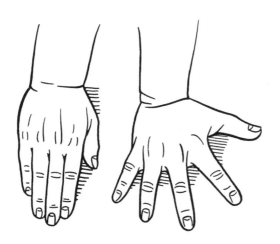

Figure 12. FINGERS
Place hand on a table or flat surface with fingers together. Then separate the fingers as widely as possible and hold. Repeat 2-3 times.

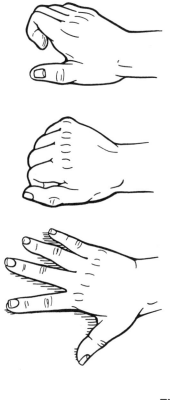

Figure 13. FINGERS
Curl the fingers tightly while keeping the knuckles straight. Complete the fist by bending the knuckles, then open the hand wide. Repeat 2-3 times.

Figure 14. HIP AND KNEE
Lying on the back, bend one knee toward the chest, then lower. Repeat with the other knee, 2-3 for times each leg.

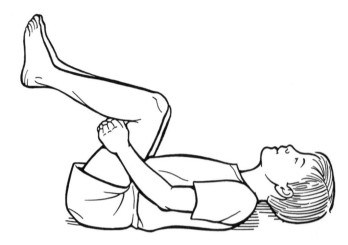

Figure 15. BACK
Lie on the back with knees bent. Keep the back flat against the floor. Raise both bent knees toward the chest. Place hands behind thighs and pull toward the chest. Lower legs to original position.

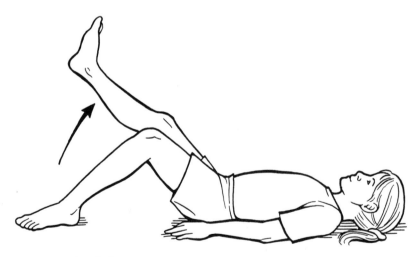

Figure 16. THIGH
Lie on the back with one leg bent at the knee and one leg straight. Raise the straight leg, keeping the knee as straight as possible. Keep the small of the back on the floor. Lower the leg and repeat with other leg.

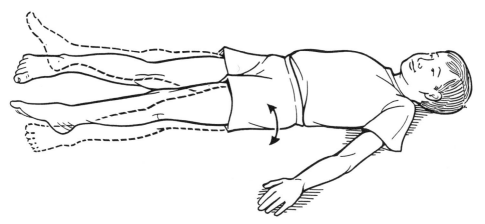

Figure 17. HIP
Lie flat on the back with legs straight, about six inches apart. Roll the legs in and out, keeping the knees straight. Repeat 2-3 times.

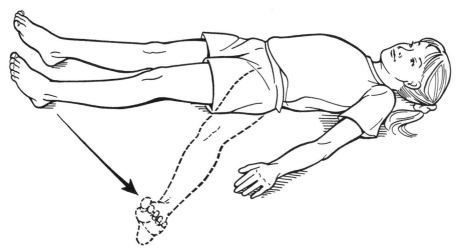

Figure 18. HIP
Lie flat on the floor with the legs straight, about six inches apart. Slide one leg out to the side and return. Repeat with the other leg. Repeat 2-3 times with each leg.

Figure 19. HIP
Lying on the stomach, lift one leg. Try to keep the knee straight.
Then lower the leg and repeat with the other leg. Repeat 2-3 times
with each leg.

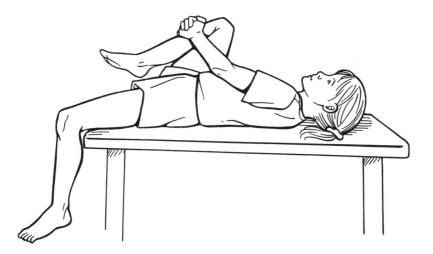

Figure 20. HIP
Lying on a table with knees bent over the edge, bring one knee up
to the chest. At the same time, keep the other thigh flat on the table.
Hold for a count of 10. Lower the leg. Repeat with the other leg.

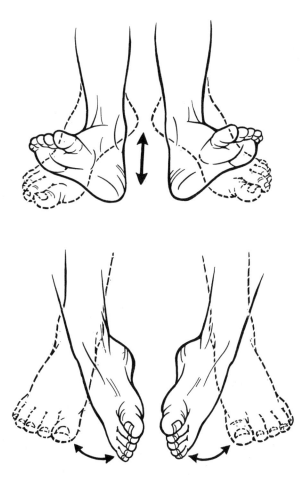

Figure 21. ANKLE

Sit in a chair with the feet on the floor. First, keeping the heels down, lift the toes up as high as possible. Then, keeping the front of the feet on the floor, lift the heels up as high as possible. Finally, turn the soles of both feet toward each other, then turn them away from each other. Repeat each movement 2-3 times.

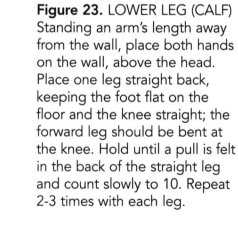

Figure 22. KNEE
Lying on the stomach, bend one knee, bringing the heel toward the buttocks. Then lower the leg and repeat with the other knee. Repeat 2-3 times with each leg.

Figure 23. LOWER LEG (CALF)
Standing an arm's length away from the wall, place both hands on the wall, above the head. Place one leg straight back, keeping the foot flat on the floor and the knee straight; the forward leg should be bent at the knee. Hold until a pull is felt in the back of the straight leg and count slowly to 10. Repeat 2-3 times with each leg.

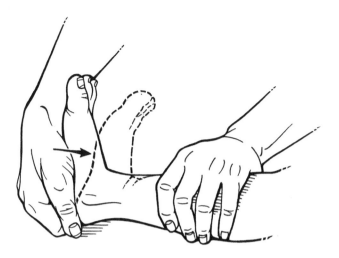

Figure 24. LOWER LEG
With your child lying on her back with her legs straight, place
your hand under her heel. Grasp her foot and lean the lower
part of your arm against the sole of her foot. Bend her foot
toward the knee, but don't use too much pressure. With your
other hand, grasp the leg between the ankle and knee to steady
the leg. Hold for a count of 10 or 15. Repeat with the other leg.

Posture

Good posture is especially important for children with arthritis, who
should be encouraged to stand, walk, sit and recline correctly. Good posture means all parts of the body should be in correct position: the spine
straight; the head upright; the shoulders gently pulled back; the chest
lifted; and the stomach and buttocks tucked in. (See Figure 25.) Slouched
or bad posture means the shoulders and upper back are rounded or
hunched, the head is forward, and the stomach is sticking out. Poor posture can cause pain and stiffness in the upper and lower back.

Encourage your child to sit in chairs that are comfortable but have a
straight, firm back. Avoid soft chairs or bean bag chairs. See that she sits
with her knees slightly higher than her hips. Her head should be back,
directly over her shoulders. (See Figure 26.) While she is sleeping or rest-

ing, make sure she uses a somewhat firm mattress with a thin pillow or no pillow at all under the head. (See Figure 27.) Pillows should not be used to prop up the knees during sleep, as this could lead to joint contractures.

How to Develop Good Posture

Figure 25. CORRECT STANDING POSTURE
The head and shoulders are back, and the chest is lifted. The buttocks are tucked under. The toes are pointed straight ahead with feet slightly apart.

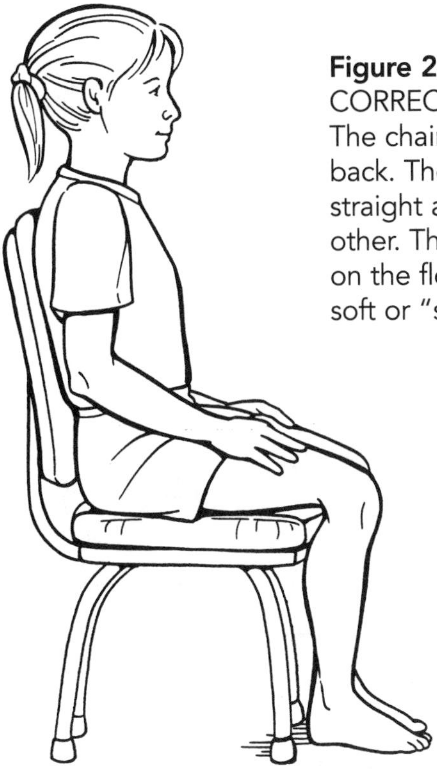

Figure 26.
CORRECT SITTING POSTURE
The chair should support the
back. The head and back are
straight and in line with each
other. The feet are placed firmly
on the floor. Avoid chairs with
soft or "sling" seats.

Figure 27. CORRECT RECLINING POSTURE
Use a firm mattress. Hold arms and legs straight.
Use a flat pillow or no pillow.

Three basic exercises can be performed to develop or maintain better posture. They are done to loosen or stretch the chest muscles at the shoulders (See Figures 28–30); firm the abdominal muscles (See Figure 31); and strengthen the muscles of the upper back (See Figure 32).

Figure 28. CHEST AND SHOULDERS
Lying on the back with a rolled towel under the head and shoulders, place hands behind head. Press elbows toward the exercise surface. Repeat 2-3 times.

Another way to develop good posture is to wear shoes that fit well and support the feet. Shoes should support the back of the foot, cushion the arch and lace up or fasten snugly. High-top shoes can help support sore ankles.

If your child's arthritis involves her feet, you might consider purchasing a second, wider pair of shoes for her to wear when her feet are swollen. This will help make her feet more comfortable. You may want to consult with a pedorthist or therapist about special shoe modifications.

Figure 29.
CHEST AND SHOULDERS
Place hands behind head.
Avoid pressing hands into
neck. Press elbows back
as far as possible, while
moving head back.
Repeat 2-3 times.

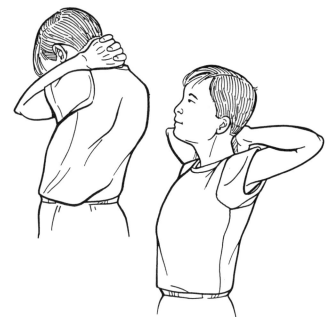

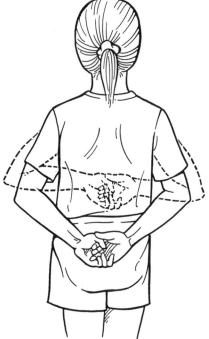

Figure 30.
CHEST AND SHOULDERS
Hold head and back erect and
place hands behind back, then
move them up to mid-back.
Return hands down to buttocks.

Figure 31. PELVIS - ABDOMEN
Lying on the back with knees bent, place hands on abdomen.
Tighten the stomach muscles and press the small of the back
into the floor. Hold and release; repeat 2-3 times.

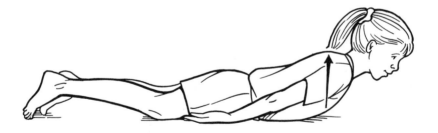

Figure 32. UPPER BACK
Lying on the stomach, lift the head and shoulders.
Hold to the count of 5 and repeat 2-3 times.

Play and Recreational Activities

"Play" involves learning and developing new skills, relating to friends and family, developing hobbies, and most of all having fun. For a child with arthritis, play activities can also help meet specific goals of treatment. Certain play activities, used with a prescribed exercise program, can help maintain normal movement in joints affected by arthritis, prevent joint misalignment, preserve muscle strength or lessen muscle weakness and maintain total body endurance and physical fitness.

Swimming and Bicycling

Swimming and bike riding are two excellent activities for children of all ages who have arthritis. Both activities help a child increase strength and endurance without causing excess stress to any joints. And both activities are almost universally popular with children.

Swimming or splashing and kicking in a swimming or wading pool allows a child to freely move her arms and legs. Water provides buoyancy (the ability to float), which makes it easier for a child with stiff joints to move. If a child doesn't know how to swim, flotation devices can be used to help her move in the water. For the child who can swim, this exercise should be greatly encouraged. Children with arthritis usually relax more easily and feel less stiff in a heated pool. Your local high school, community center or YMCA may have swimming pools available. You'll find that your child will do better if she has a regularly scheduled time to swim with friends or family. Many children with arthritis are able to participate on swim teams.

Bicycling can help maintain joint mobility and muscle strength in the legs. It also builds endurance. It is important that the bike's seat and handlebars be adjusted appropriately for the size of your child. If your child is too young to ride a bicycle, she can use a tricycle, which also can be useful for a child who is unable to walk during a flare.

Limits or Restrictions to Consider

Your child should be given every chance to play with friends and to participate in games and other enjoyable activities. Help your child choose games or sports that are appropriate for her age and physical condition.

It is wise to discuss the appropriateness of your child's participation in sports and other activities with her doctor or therapist. Children usually stop playing when they feel tired, although sometimes they may push themselves too hard or too far to keep up with friends. It is important for children to learn to pace their activities.

You and the doctor should help your child choose activities or sports that are safe and fun. Some activities may be fine for one child but too intense for another. Here are some general guidelines; how closely your child should follow them will depend on the extent of her disease involvement and the recommendations of her doctor. Enforcing these restrictions will come up each year in the school environment; Chapter 10 will address school concerns.

- Avoid games and sports that put stress on joints affected by arthritis. These include gymnastics, basketball, volleyball, high impact aerobic dancing, jumping rope and hopscotch.

- Avoid activities such as soccer or track that require a child to walk or run for a long period of time if your child has significant arthritis in her legs or feet.

- Avoid contact sports such as football or hockey, which may put too much stress on the joints.

Recreational Activities for a Young Child

Playing with toys in the bathtub. This helps a child exercise her arms and legs, and the warm water helps relieve stiffness or pain.

Playing "Simon Says." This encourages a child to move any joints in the neck, back, arms or legs that may be affected by arthritis. For example, you might say: "Simon says reach for the ceiling." This game can be used to have a child bend or straighten every major joint in the body.

Dancing to music. Many young children enjoy freedom of movement and expression when they are encouraged to dance to their favorite tunes.

Play Activities for Movement of the Legs and Feet

Kicking the ball. This can help straighten out the knee. Roll a soft, light kickball toward your child (she may be as young as two) and have her kick it back to you.

Walking backward on heels. This can help straighten out the knee, and can aid ankle bending. Most children can do this by the time they are four or five.

Tag or "red light/green light." These are simple running games that require short distance running for brief periods.

Roller skating or ice skating. With the help of kneepads and wrist guards, these activities can be enjoyed by many young children with arthritis. Those with hand or wrist involvement may want to avoid skating, since hands often take the brunt of a fall.

Dance and ballet. With some modifications, dance and ballet are helpful in stretching and strengthening muscles and joints. Consult your child's doctor or physical therapist before enrolling her in a dance class or program; be sure to discuss her physical limitations with the teacher ahead of time.

Play Activities for Movement of the Hands and Arms

The following are good activities for hand and arm movement: catching or batting away a balloon; using "play dough" or modeling clay; pretending to do housework, such as dusting or sweeping; coloring; drawing; finger painting; cutting and pasting.

Recreational Activities for Older Children and Teenagers

As children grow and develop, they enjoy taking part in organized games and sports. Learning about personal and group efforts can be life-long benefits of these activities. Activities such as competitive swimming and water polo are great team sports for children with arthritis. Be sure the team's coach understands your child's abilities and limitations.

Most of the activities suggested in this manual give the older child a chance to improve or maintain joint motion, balance, coordination, muscle strength and overall physical fitness. Keep in mind that sports activities will not replace the prescribed exercise program, because they do not require the full range of motion of all joints of the body. Your child should know how to warm up and stretch before playing any vigorous game and how to cool down after a physical activity.

Some children with arthritis may not be able to participate fully in physical education classes or contact sports. You can work with your child's physical education teacher to adapt the activities so she can participate. They should also be encouraged to get involved as scorekeepers, timekeepers, managers, trainers, referees or umpires.

Activities that a child can do by herself include running or walking short distances, biking, rowing a boat, playing a musical instrument, learning sign language or participating in crafts.

Suggested group activities and team sports include kickball, dodgeball, tag, hide-and-seek, kick the can, modern dance, softball, baseball, gentle tumbling, badminton, table tennis, paddleball and golf.

There are many other physical activities that are fun and beneficial in maintaining your child's overall health status. Check with your child's doctor or therapist for more options.

Summary

Regular movement helps keep your child's joints flexible. A daily exercise program that takes each of her affected joints through their full range of motion will lessen stiffness, loss of motion and misalignment. Certain play activities, used in conjunction with a prescribed exercise program, can help maintain movement and strength, as well as maintain total body endurance and physical fitness.

Pain Assessment and Management

What Is Pain?

As the parent of a child with juvenile arthritis, you are in a unique position to help your child deal with her disease. No doubt you have figured out many effective ways of helping your child cope with pain. You might prepare a hot bath to soothe your child's aches and pains or read her a story to help take her mind off the pain. This chapter can help you understand how pain works and provide you with some practical approaches to helping your child deal with pain. You will read about a variety of techniques known as "cognitive-behavioral" methods of pain management.

Understanding Pain

Pain is the body's alarm system, signaling when something is wrong. When part of the body is injured or damaged, nerves in that area release chemical signals. The nerves act like tiny telephone wires and send these signals to your brain, where they are recognized as pain. This process stimulates the formation and release of endorphins (naturally-occurring painkilling substances).

Pain "tells" you that you need to do something. For example, the intense pain you feel when you touch a hot stove tells you to pull your hand away to prevent further injury. Likewise, a swollen, acutely painful joint during a flare is a signal to rest the joint and allow it to recover.

The long-lasting, chronic pain of arthritis is different; it's a stubborn, lower-key general distress signal that is more difficult to interpret. There is no magic solution to getting rid of chronic pain, but it can be managed with rest, medications, relaxation, exercise and other strategies. Think of your pain as a signal to take action, rather than an ordeal to be endured.

Please heed two important cautions about the pain management strategies explained here. First, they are not intended to be a substitute for the medical treatments your child is receiving. Your child should continue taking any medications prescribed to treat symptoms, including pain. This program is meant to be used in addition to medical treatments your child is receiving.

The second caution is a very important point that is easily misunderstood. Although this chapter will describe how thoughts and feelings are involved in the experience of pain, it is by no means suggesting that the pain is "all in your child's head." Pain is neither all "in the body" (which is what some people label as "real" pain), or all "in the mind" (which some people dismiss as not "real"). Instead, the mind and body are interconnected and interacting parts of the whole person. Just as coming down with a cold can influence our emotions (we feel cranky and more easily upset), so can a major worry or anxiety lead to some physical discomfort (for example, we get a headache or upset stomach when we are worried about some important event in our lives). The best approach to pain management is to consider the whole person and try to identify which factors – physical, emotional or cognitive – can be modified to reduce the effect pain has on your child's life.

You have probably heard amazing stories about people who have experienced severe injuries but have felt little or no pain until minutes or even hours later. Common examples are sports-related injuries: a football player who doesn't notice that he has a broken rib until after the game is over. This illustrates an important fact about pain: There are processes within the body and mind that can change the experience and perception of pain.

This is an important point, because it challenges the myth that there is a direct cause and effect relationship between the severity of injury or tissue damage and the amount of pain that the person experiences. In that view of pain, the same injury will produce the same amount of pain in every person. This simply isn't true. But if there isn't such a direct relationship between injury or tissue damage and pain, what factors *are* involved in the experience of pain? An easy way to understand the interplay of these factors is to think of them as parts of a puzzle made up of a person's nervous system signals, feelings, thoughts and behavior. When you fit all the pieces together you have a more complete picture of the pain experience (see Figure 33). This concept, developed by Michael Rapoff, PhD, at the University of Kansas Medical Center in Kansas City, is described in more detail below.

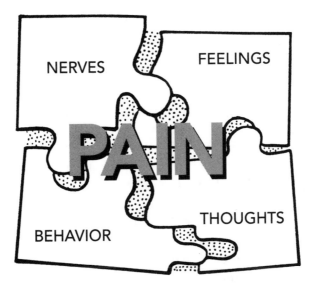

Figure 33. THE PAIN PUZZLE

The Pain Puzzle

Puzzle Piece #1: The Signals of the Nervous System

When nerves are stimulated by some type of injury or damage to the body, they transmit signals that our brain defines as "pain". The experience of pain begins when nerve fibers translate heat, mechanical pressure or chemical irritants into sensory signals. For instance, the stretching and swelling of arthritis inflammation in a joint puts increased pressure on nearby nerve fibers. These sensory signals are transmitted through a series of relay points, called synapses, until they finally reach the brain. At the same time, there are messages coming "down" from the brain via the same relay points. These descending signals can modify the incoming pain signals, thus changing the sensation of pain.

One example of how these up and down signals work together is found in what some people refer to as the "runner's high." Many people who do long-distance running (or other prolonged vigorous exercise) report that at a certain point a sense of euphoria replaces the pain that they were feeling only moments earlier. Research has shown that this euphoria is due to chemical substances called "endorphins" that are released into the nervous system by the descending sensory processes. In effect, this chemical acts as a naturally produced pain reliever.

There are other examples of these down processes that are very important for the management of pain. These other processes involve more cognitive (thinking) and affective (emotional) factors. For example, the amount of attention you focus on the sensory signals and whether you have positive or negative feelings can influence how the brain interprets the sensory signals it receives. The other pieces of the pain puzzle will examine these factors in more detail.

Puzzle Piece #2: Affective Responses (Feelings)

There is a very close relationship between pain and emotional responses, particularly depression. People who have chronic pain are more likely to experience depression, and people who are depressed are more likely to experience some type of chronic pain problem. Treating either pain or depression can often result in relief from both.

Yet trying to determine whether pain causes depression or depression causes pain can be unproductive. Some researchers suggest that the reason pain and depression go together so often is that sensory signals from the body connect with both pain centers and emotion centers in the brain. Other researchers don't agree with this idea and point out that not all people who experience pain also feel depressed. They believe that there are some processes that must occur between pain and depression in order for emotional upset to be a result of pain problems.

Regardless of whether pain causes depression or vice versa, there is often a negative cycle. Pain sensations can prevent the child from continuing a particular favorite activity; this can cause emotional upset (frustration, anger, sadness) and behavioral isolation, which in turn can lead to overall decreased activity levels. Decreased activity can then lead to decreased fitness levels, which can contribute to more, or more intense, pain sensations.

Sadness and depression are not the only emotional reactions that may accompany the pain experience. Other emotions that can also be connected to pain include fear, worry and anger. A teenager with arthritis may worry that increased pain means that her disease is getting worse, and may limit future activities and plans. A child may be angry about having to deal with the negative effects of having a chronic disease, and this anger can cause increased muscle tension and pain.

Puzzle Piece #3: Cognitive Processes (Thoughts)

Our thought processes also play a part in the pain experience. Human beings attempt to understand and attach meaning to their experiences, even when those experiences are physical sensations from one's own body. When we have headaches, we may wonder if they are the result of fatigue, eye strain, too much coffee or stress. The way we attach meaning to or interpret our experiences has to do with several thinking-related or cognitive factors, including beliefs, attitudes, coping self-talk (what we say to ourselves) and attention focus.

The beliefs we hold about pain play an important role in the pain experience. Beliefs about the cause of the pain, the course it will take in the future, the treatments that will be needed, our own ability to cope with the pain, as well as beliefs about whether we are helpless in the face of pain or whether we can do things to help ourselves, will all affect the experience.

Several attitudes or expectations about ourselves and others can influence the pain experience. For example, the attitude that you should be "tough" and never express pain, that having pain means you can't function normally, or that you need others to express a lot of sympathy to deal with the pain can all play a role in the pain experience.

Coping self-talk has to do with what we say to ourselves about pain. Sometimes our thoughts are negative or unhelpful and can be described as "catastrophizing," or thinking that the pain is "terrible," "unbearable," "overwhelming," or "unmanageable." In contrast, thoughts can be positive or helpful, such as viewing pain as "tolerable," "bearable," and "manageable." Also, how one focuses attention can influence the pain experience. You have probably been able to distract your child by reading, playing a board game, coloring or talking to her, which helped take her mind off the pain.

Puzzle Piece #4: Behavior

Your child's behavior and your own behavior are important parts of the pain puzzle. When your child is in pain, he or she may display "pain behaviors," such as limping, grimacing, crying, resting or asking for pain medication. These behaviors are important and provide clues to how your child is feeling. It is helpful to notice these behaviors so that you can report them to your child's doctor and take necessary steps to help your child.

How you respond to your child's pain behaviors directly influences how she copes with her pain. If you encourage her to take prescribed medications and use coping strategies, she will cope better with pain, suffer less and be less limited by the pain. However, if you respond to your child's pain only with sympathy but do not encourage her to actively cope with the pain, she will cope more poorly and suffer more negative consequences from the pain. Generally speaking, children with arthritis do not try to take advantage of their disease or the pain they feel just to get more attention or avoid chores or other undesirable activities. By encouraging your child to be as active as possible and by focusing on positive coping efforts, you can reduce the likelihood that she will let the pain be an excuse for not participating in activities.

Some Practical Approaches to Dealing with Pain

The Power of Positive Thinking

The Pain Puzzle concept illustrates how important emotions and feelings can be in coping with pain. Children who feel helpless and depressed about their condition tend to decrease their activity, develop a poor self-esteem and, not surprisingly, feel worse.

Learning to think differently may not get rid of your child's pain entirely, but having a more positive attitude can help. Also, your child takes cues from you, so how *you* feel about your child's illness can have a significant impact on how she feels.

It's easy for someone with a chronic health problem to slip into a life built around pain and sickness. Instead of focusing on illness, help your child devote her attention to health instead. Help her think of arthritis management as pursuing health rather than fighting illness.

Help your child develop interests and hobbies that engross her and help take her mind off pain. The more she concentrates on something outside her body, the less she'll be aware of physical discomfort. Likewise, laughter really is good medicine. A sense of humor can be a powerful antidote to pain.

Relaxation

Learning to relax – really relax – gives your child a sense of control and well-being that makes pain easier to manage. Relaxation is more than just sitting down to read or watch TV. It involves learning to calm and control your body and mind. Like swimming or using a computer, relaxation is a skill that must be practiced.

When your child wants to fall asleep, the following techniques can help her relax enough to become drowsy. They can also be used at other times of the day to reduce stress, pain and tension, and to give her more energy.

One of the simplest ways for your child to learn to relax is to tense (tighten) and then relax one muscle group at a time, moving from her toes to her head. Ask her to hold the muscles tight for 5-10 seconds, then let the muscles relax. As they relax, tell her to become aware of tension drifting away. Encourage her to take slow, deep breaths, then blow the air out completely. At this point, she should begin feeling relaxed. If she feels any pain, try the following methods of relaxing.

First, create a quiet, calm setting. Depending on the age of your child, this could be her room (but without telephone, TV, stereo or other distractions.) Tell her to concentrate on a favorite picture, activity, place or toy, and ask her not to think about anything else, except that favorite relaxing image. After about 10 minutes of deep breathing, your child should start to feel calm and relaxed.

Most health professionals can instruct your child on relaxation techniques. Many books and audiotapes are available as well. Ask your doctor or other health-care team members, such as a physical therapist, for more ways to teach your child how to relax and determine which methods work best. At first, you should practice them with your child. Then encourage her to practice them alone so they are easy for her to do.

Heat and Cold Treatments

Heat and cold are both very helpful for the relief of pain and stiffness. They relax muscles and reduce inflammation around joints, thus allowing ease of movement. Heat and cold provide only temporary relief, however, and should not replace medication or exercise.

Using Heat Treatments

Here are some examples of heat treatments:

- Warm baths, taken in the morning, can reduce stiffness and enable your child to get ready for school.

- Hot packs, applied to painful joints, can make them more flexible and less painful. Hot packs are gel-filled bags that are heated in hot water or in a microwave, covered with a dry towel, and placed on the joint. They are available at most drug stores. Towels soaked in hot water can also serve as hot packs. Hydrocollator packs, canvas bags that contain silicone gel, retain heat for an even longer time. They can be purchased at drug stores and at medical supply stores.

- Paraffin baths distribute heat evenly around the small joints. This treatment is useful for children who have arthritis in their hands and feet. Small portable paraffin units for home use are available.

They use a mixture of paraffin and oil that is kept at a properly controlled temperature at all times. The hand (or sometimes the foot) is dipped into the bath 10-12 times, until a thick coating forms. Then the hand or foot is wrapped in plastic and covered with a towel for about 20 minutes. The upkeep of the paraffin unit is easy. Ask your physical therapist for information about its use and effectiveness. Follow the usual precautions for using electrical devices.

Other ways to loosen stiff muscles with heat include:

- Sleeping under an electric blanket or on a heated mattress pad can help reduce morning stiffness and pain. If your child uses an electric blanket, you might help her avoid morning stiffness by turning the blanket up 15-30 minutes before it is time for her to get up. Or place a sleeping bag on top of the regular bed to provide a kind of cocoon of warmth.

- A hot water bottle wrapped in a towel can be placed on or under a painful joint while the child sleeps.

- Some children benefit from a heated waterbed. A flotation mattress can help in the same way, and isn't as heavy as a waterbed. It's all right for your child to use these, but be careful – a waterbed or flotation mattress could potentially make hip problems worse. (Check with a physical therapist to make sure a waterbed or flotation mattress won't worsen your child's contractures. The therapist can teach your child how to position herself in bed. Otherwise, she will probably put her joints in their most comfortable position – most likely flexed – which could lead to contractures.)

- A down quilt or duvet is lightweight and cozy and can provide a lot of warmth. Flannel sheets feel warmer than cotton in the winter. To ease morning stiffness, you might try warming your child's clothes by putting them in the dryer for a few minutes (and her shoes on top of the dryer) before she puts them on.

Using Cold Treatments

Cold can also be effective in providing relief from pain. Cold packs can be purchased in stores or can be made by simply filling plastic bags with ice cubes or using packs of frozen vegetables and wrapping the bag in a thin towel or cloth. Apply the bag to the area for no longer than 10 minutes. A freezer pack that has been slightly thawed can be used to wrap around your child's fingers. It can then be refrozen and used again. These freezer packs can be bought at discount stores or drugstores.

A Word About Safety

Follow these safety tips when using heat and cold techniques for pain relief:

- Use only on dry, healthy skin.

- Protect your child's skin by putting a towel between her skin and any type of hot or cold pack.

- Treat each area for only 15 to 20 minutes at a time. Let the skin return to normal body temperature before another application.

- Don't apply heat or cold treatments to any area of the body in which circulation is poor.

- Don't let your child lie on top of an electric heating pad or blanket.

- Don't use any electrical device that is not UL (Underwriter's Laboratory) approved and in good repair.

Sleep, Rest and Energy Conservation

Because your child has arthritis, she may need more sleep and rest than other children her age. Keep in mind that a well-rested body is a healthier, stronger body. If your child has trouble falling asleep, discourage her from having any drinks or foods that contain caffeine (colas, chocolate bars) before bedtime. Caffeine can make it hard to fall asleep. For older children who have trouble falling asleep, relaxation methods (described on p. 69) can be quite helpful. If pain is severe enough to prevent your child from sleeping, talk to your physician.

Children with arthritis often feel tired and lack the energy to stay active throughout the day. That's why it's necessary for them to use their strength and energy wisely. Explain to your child that it is important to rest when she starts to get tired. If she becomes exhausted, she will have to rest longer to make up for it.

The ideal rest is a nap on a firm bed, but don't try to force sleep. Rather, create a "quiet" time each day when your child can relax and fall asleep when she becomes drowsy. Older children can be taught that a 20-minute or longer rest period in midday or late afternoon often allows them to do more in a given day, so they are not "dragging" through the rest of the day tired.

Here are some ways you can help your child conserve energy and get the rest she needs:

- Teach your child to recognize the signals from her body that mean it's time to rest. Encourage her to know or sense her limits.

- Help your child pace her activities. Alternating heavy and light activities helps prevent fatigue. For example, reading a book or drawing in a coloring book after playing an active outdoor game will help maintain energy and prevent exhaustion.

- Set priorities. If your child has a lot of homework and chores, have her do the most important activities first and save the others to do when she is rested. You can help your child learn to set priorities so that everything gets done.

- Plan ahead. Decide with your child what needs to be done; then make a list or a schedule.

- Make chores and work simpler. By sitting to work when possible, or sitting on the bed while getting dressed, your child can stretch her supply of energy. Remember to have her move around periodically when she is sitting for long periods of time to prevent stiffness.

- Get help when needed. Teach your child that it is okay to ask for assistance. Sometimes a friend or sibling can reach for an object or carry a package, especially if he or she understands why it's important to help.

Supporting the Joints with Splints

The doctor or therapist may recommend that your child wear splints.
There are two reasons why splints may be helpful:

- Splints provide rest and support to muscles and inflamed joints.

- Splints can help prevent or reduce joint misalignment, and as a
  result can preserve your child's range of motion.

Misalignments can develop during sleep and at rest, when a child's
joints tend to bend into their most comfortable positions. For that
reason, splints are only worn at night in most cases. A plastic splint,
designed just for your child by the therapist, can help keep joints in
their most functional position.

Some children don't want to wear a splint, because it may feel awkward
and uncomfortable at first. Others feel very relaxed wearing them, because
they don't have to worry about trying to keep their arms or legs straight.
Help your child understand why wearing her splint is important. Remind
her that the splint will hold the joint in a position that might reduce pain,
and that wearing it now may prevent having to do so in the future.
Encourage her to take responsibility for wearing her splint properly.

Remember to have your child bring her splint when she visits the
doctor or therapist. To work well, a splint must fit properly, so it needs
to be checked when you return for subsequent visits. Most splints can
be revised as movement in the joints improves.

Considering Alternative, Complementary and Unproven Remedies

Outside your child's doctor's office lies a wide range of treatments and
therapies not covered under the umbrella of conventional medicine.
Some, like massage, aromatherapy or yoga, may be useful in promoting
relaxation or alleviating pain. Others may or may not do anything at all.
And still others – like large doses of vitamins or certain herbs – can be
downright harmful.

Whether a treatment is "complementary" or "alternative" depends on how you use it. That is, if you discuss a particular treatment with your child's doctor and learn that it cannot harm your child, then use it in conjunction with your child's medical treatment plan, it's complementary. It may or may not help, but it certainly won't hurt.

If you use the proposed treatment as an alternative to your child's ongoing medical treatment plan, it's an "alternative" treatment. This type of approach can be harmful to your child because she will not be getting the proven medical treatment she needs. If proper medication isn't taken, exercises aren't done, and joint protection isn't practiced, your child can develop some serious problems that may not be easy to correct.

Treatments without sufficient scientific data to show that they are safe and effective are called "unproven remedies." Some of these remedies are new treatments still under study. They are considered experimental until repeated, controlled studies show that they work and won't cause any harm. Others are health frauds with no scientific basis for their claims. These can be dangerous to your child's health and harmful to your checkbook as well.

Parents of children with chronic pain can be prime targets for health fraud promoters because of the hope that a new treatment will be discovered. Be particularly wary of anything labeled as a cure. Rest assured that when a significant medical advance is made, it will be reported in reputable scientific journals and your doctor will know about it. There is no secret cure for arthritis and, in fact, there will never be just one cure for the many different kinds of arthritis.

Your best bet is to discuss any additional treatment you are considering with your child's doctor. If your doctor assures you the treatment cannot cause any harm and you feel its potential benefits justify the expense, then try it out *in addition to* your child's medical treatment program. Remember, though, that arthritis has an unpredictable nature. Sometimes it seems to go away completely (remission); other times it gets worse (flares). This changing course makes it difficult to know if a treatment is actually helping or if the arthritis just happened to improve on its own.

QUESTIONS TO ASK ABOUT COMPLEMENTARY TREATMENTS

- Was the treatment tested in studies set up according to good scientific principles?

- Did the studies use a control group for comparison (a group of people who did not receive the treatment)? Without a control group, there is no proof that the treatment in question was the cause of any improvement.

- Were any positive findings confirmed by studies at other research centers?

- Was the treatment tested on people, not just animals?

- Were there any harmful effects?

BE SUSPICIOUS OF ANY TREATMENT THAT

- Promises a cure. (Anyone who claims to be able to cure your child's arthritis is most likely much more interested in your money than in your child's health.)

- Claims that standard medical treatment is not effective.

- Does not list the beneficial ingredients.

- Relies on case histories or testimonials as proof of its effectiveness.

- Is available from only one source.

Remember, anything that sounds too good to be true probably is.

Office Procedures,
Surgery and Hospitalization

Office Procedures

During the course of her treatment, your child is likely to have several different tests or procedures performed. You can help prepare her by learning about them yourself. Ask the doctor what will happen to your child before, during and afterward and find out what you should do to help.

Some of the tests and office procedures your child is most likely to experience are:

Blood Tests
A blood sample is taken from a vein in the forearm and tested sometimes to measure the degree of inflammation, or determine if there is damage to an organ such as the liver.

Urine Tests
These tests may be needed to measure the effects of certain medications. They also can alert the doctor to any kidney damage.

Joint Fluid Tests

A needle is placed in the joint and fluid is withdrawn. The fluid can then be studied to measure inflammatory activity. The fluid is sometimes cultured (grown in a special substance) to check for bacteria.

X-rays or Bone Scans

These may be taken of your child's bones from time to time to check for possible damage, and to determine if the bones are growing normally.

Joint Injection

Occasionally a joint, usually the knee, that has been resistant to treatment with medications will be injected with glucocorticoids.

Surgery

Most children with arthritis will never have surgery for their arthritis. Often the disease becomes inactive, leaving no permanent joint damage. However, for some children – those whose disease remains active and who have significant joint damage – surgery may be an option.

Most of the time, proper exercise, stretching and the use of splints prevent joint contractures. However, when contractures resist treatment, surgery is sometimes needed. In one such procedure, called a soft tissue release, the surgeon cuts the tight tissues that caused the contracture, restoring movement. With proper physical therapy, many children discover that they can move and bend joints that once were "frozen."

Arthroscopic surgery allows the surgeon to view and operate inside the joint, using a very thin tube with a light at the end. This is sometimes done when a joint, usually the knee, is very painful and unstable. Usually bone chips are gently removed through the tube by suction.

Synovectomy is the removal of inflamed tissue from the lining of a joint. It is sometimes performed when the pain and swelling of a joint is severe and not responsive to medications or local injections.

Once done only rarely in children, joint replacement surgery is now more common in older children. In this procedure, the surgeon removes the damaged joint and replaces it with a man-made implant. Before any

older child or young adult agrees to this procedure, she needs to understand what is involved, how long the replacement will last, and what
will be expected of her before and after surgery, including a vigorous
program of special exercises.

QUESTIONS TO ASK THE DOCTOR WHEN CONSIDERING SURGERY

- What type of surgery is being considered?

- What will happen if the surgery isn't performed or is delayed? Are there any other possible options?

- What are the potential benefits versus the risks of this surgery?

- What will happen before, during and after the operation?

- How long will the operation last? How soon can I see my child after surgery?

- How long will my child be in the hospital? Out of school?

- How much pain will she have afterwards?

- Will my child need to alter her medication before or after surgery?

- How much therapy will be needed before and after surgery?

- What equipment or supplies will be needed at home?

- How much will the surgery cost? Will my insurance pay for it?

- What side effects of surgery may occur and how likely are they?

- How long will the benefits from surgery last?

- For joint replacement surgery, might arthritis return to the joint? After joint replacement surgery, will the new joint wear out or slip at some time? What are the possible complications of joint replacement surgery for someone my child's age?

Preparing Your Child

Depending on your child's age and prior experience with a hospital, you will want to inform and reassure her as much as possible. First, deal with her fears and questions by telling her in simple language what is going to happen.

Don't forget to also explain to her why she is going into the hospital. Tell her, for instance, that surgery is needed to help her hip or knee so she'll be able to move it better. Continue to answer her questions and listen to her fears. Make sure she knows that going to the hospital isn't punishment for anything she has done. Try to talk to her honestly and simply, even about unpleasant parts. Explain that she will be asleep during surgery and that she will wake up later. Try not to hold back information – your child can sense it if you do. If you don't know the answer to a question, tell her you don't know, and find out. Encourage her to also ask questions of the staff.

When Your Child Is Hospitalized

All parents are concerned about their children's welfare during a hospital stay. A key point is to communicate with the hospital staff. Just as you have become used to talking openly with other members of your child's health-care team, try to be open and honest with hospital staff. Make a list of your questions or concerns, and ask them of the staff. It is your right and responsibility to be informed.

If your child is to have surgery, be sure you and your child talk with the doctor about pain medication. You want to make sure adequate pain medication is available so your child will be as comfortable as possible after any procedure. Don't hesitate to alert the doctors and nurses to any special problems your child has. For example, if your child will be under general anesthesia (asleep) for surgery, and she has limited mobility in her neck, make sure you tell the anesthesiologist or anesthetist so they can be careful to avoid forcing the neck farther than it should go.

If you are concerned about the care your child is receiving, tell a nurse or your doctor, rather than keeping the complaint to yourself. By the same token, if you feel your child is receiving thoughtful, sensitive, loving care, tell the staff. Your feedback helps the staff learn about caring for children with arthritis. Your comments can help provide better care for other hospitalized children in the future.

Keep in mind that you know your child better than anyone else. You have valuable information about her past experiences with medications, bed rest, splinting, exercise, activities and moods. All of this information needs to be shared. Doing so will help make certain your child receives the finest care possible. It will also make you feel that you have done your part.

Besides supplying simple, concrete information there are several things you can do to boost your child's spirits and calm her fears about being hospitalized. Here are a few tips:

- Tell the hospital staff members your child's nickname, and ask that they use it.

- If it's allowed, bring some of your child's familiar things from home, such as a favorite blanket, pajamas, slippers, toys, stuffed animals, coloring books, crayons, storybooks and so on. For older children, books, magazines and a radio may be just as important. Anything familiar will make her feel more secure, less lonesome, and will help relieve her pain and fears.

- Tell your child exactly when you will be with her and when you'll be away from her. For a preschool child, separation from parents and family is usually the most frightening part of the hospital experience.

- If your child is going to be in the hospital for more than a few days, urge other family members and friends to visit her.

- Take advantage of any programs, parties or tours that are available to acquaint children with the hospital. Usually, children are encouraged to observe the operating rooms and recovery areas, and are permitted to touch the equipment or hospital gowns. Information about anesthesia and recovery are usually explained.

- Before going to the hospital, ask your child how she feels about it. Is there anything she dreads? If there is, you might be able to help soothe her fears. For example, if she is terrified of needles, you could encourage her to pretend she is giving a stuffed animal a shot to help her work out some of her fear or hostility. This is called therapeutic play.

- Before your child enters the hospital, ask what she thinks will happen. If she's wrong about something, you can clarify that point so there will be few surprises.

- Stay calm. If you communicate well with the staff and your child, you will have done all you can to see that your child's needs are met. Your calmness and confidence will help ease your child's hospital experience.

Activities of Daily Living

Joint Protection

To maintain function and mobility, your child needs to be physically active. At the same time, joints with arthritis need to be protected from overuse and abuse, which can lead to swelling, joint damage and loss of function. By encouraging your child to learn and use joint protection techniques, you can help her get into the habit of protecting her joints. Here are some ideas; ask your child's doctor or therapist for more suggestions.

- Have your child change positions often to avoid stiffness. Encourage your child to get up and walk or stretch whenever she's been sitting for a long time. Make sure she knows to stretch and bend her fingers from time to time before she gets stiff from writing, drawing or coloring.

- Have her avoid activities that require a tight grip or that put pressure on her fingers. Build up her pencils, crayons and pens with foam rubber (the "sponge" sometimes used in hair curlers works) so that she doesn't need a tight grip that use them. Wide-diameter pens and pencils are available, as are grips that slide over standard writing tools.

• Suggest that she use a backpack rather than a bookbag for school items. A backpack can be worn on both shoulders to distribute weight evenly, thereby preventing undue stress.

• If possible, obtain an extra set of school books to keep at home. That way, your child won't have to carry heavy books back and forth between home and school.

• Encourage her to use her larger or stronger joints to reduce stress on smaller and weaker ones; have her push or slide heavy objects rather than try to lift or carry them.

• If she has to lift or carry something, have her use both arms or hands to support the weight, instead of just one. For example, encourage her to carry her lunch tray with both forearms under the tray for support.

• Encourage her to maintain good posture. Shoulders should be kept back, tummy in, and head up when standing or sitting. (For more information about correct posture, refer to page 53.)

Making Daily Activities Easier

The more everyday activities your child can do on her own, the healthier and happier she is likely to be. Getting herself out of bed in the morning and bathing, dressing and eating without help builds your child's independence, confidence and self-esteem.

Though most children will need some help every now and then, older children can usually handle these basic tasks by themselves. Many self-help devices can be bought or made to make tasks easier. The following sections list some tips for making daily activities easier. Ask your child's occupational therapist for more ideas.

Bathing and Grooming

- Get your child up early enough to allow plenty of time to get everything done without feeling rushed. (This may mean instituting an earlier bedtime.)

- Suggest that she take a morning bath or shower to help decrease morning stiffness. If possible, run the bath water ahead of time so warm water is waiting when she arises.

- If needed, install grab bars near the tub and toilet to ensure that she doesn't slip or fall.

- Place a nonslip bathmat in the tub to help prevent falls.

- If you have one, suggest that it may be easier to use a walk-in shower, rather than a tub shower.

- Place a shower bench in the back of a tub shower so she can sit while showering.

- Provide her with long-handled brushes and combs, with the handles built up with foam rubber. A long-handled brush can help her bathe her feet and other parts of her body if her reach is limited.

- Supply her with a bath pillow to make soaking in the bathtub more comfortable, and a towel mitt to aid in washing and drying.

- Show her how to squeeze toothpaste with the palm of her hand onto a toothbrush, rather than straining sore fingers. Or try the pump bottles of toothpaste that are available.

- To make thorough teeth cleaning easier, buy an electric toothbrush with a built-up handle.

Dressing

- Encourage her to choose what she is going to wear the next day at night, so her clothes are ready and waiting in the morning.

- Shop for clothes that are easy to put on and take off. Loose-fitting garments with front openings are usually easiest, and Velcro fasteners or snaps are simpler to handle than buttons.

- Provide her with low, easy-to-reach shelves for storing clothes and shoes. Use a low bar for hanging clothes.

- Try adding rings to her zippers to make them easier to pull.

- Attach cloth loops to socks so they can be pulled on more easily.

- If your child has foot involvement, buy athletic shoes with Velcro fasteners, or similar slip-on shoes that are easy to put on but still provide adequate support. She might try using elastic shoelaces in shoes and leaving them tied so she can slip her feet into them more easily.

- Buy a long-handled shoehorn to help her put on shoes.

Eating

- Build up handles on forks, knives and spoons so they are easier to grasp. Or buy a set of utensils with large handles for the whole family to use. This helps your child feel less different and isolated.

- Use lightweight utensils and dishes, which are easy to handle.

- Provide lightweight mugs or cups with large handles.

- Show her how to use both hands to hold a cup or glass, spreading the fingers all the way around.

- Provide her with a flexible straw if she has difficulty holding a cup.

- Place a rubber disk or a damp cloth under her dishes at the dinner table to keep them in place.

Figure 34. FOOD GUIDE PYRAMID

Diet and Nutrition

Your child needs to eat a balanced, nutritious diet to be as healthy as she can be and to maintain a healthy body weight. She should eat a varied, well-balanced diet that consists primarily of grains, fruits and vegetables. The Food Guide Pyramid, (see Figure 34) developed by the U.S. Department of Agriculture and Health and Human Services, shows how to make wise food choices that will provide your child with the nutrients she needs for energy, strength and growth. Select most foods from the bottom two layers of the pyramid and fewer foods from the top.

Since 1994, a comprehensive nutrition label has been required for most food products, so it is easier for consumers to know how much fat, sodium or cholesterol they are actually getting. Information on these labels can help you make smart choices for a healthier diet. Because of the medications they take, some children may need to limit sodium intake and increase their folic acid and calcium intake.

There's no magic rule to eating three meals a day, and nutritious snacks are very important for children and should be encouraged. If your child eats several small meals each day, that's all right as long as she gets the nutrients needed.

At this time, there is no known diet cure for childhood arthritis. From time to time there have been personal reports of improvement from eating or avoiding certain foods. However, there has never been any consistent pattern that would prompt doctors to suggest that children with arthritis should eat or avoid any particular foods.

Don't be persuaded by ads to try a fad diet or vitamins and nutritional supplements that claim to be cures for arthritis. Rather, see that your child eats proper foods. Ask your doctor or a dietitian (a specialist in nutrition) for suggestions.

When the disease is active and your child does not feel well, she may not have an appetite. Her medication may cause weight gain or loss of appetite. If your child doesn't want to eat, try some different eating schedules. Be creative and try to make meals special family events.

Chronic illness and poor eating habits can both lead to anemia, a reduction in the red blood cells that causes extreme tiredness. Lack of weight bearing on sore joints can cause thinning and weakening of the bones, or osteoporosis. Medications, including glucocorticoids like prednisone, can worsen this condition. Because of these bone problems, the doctor may prescribe calcium supplements for your child.

If your child is overweight, ask the doctor or dietitian to suggest a diet that will give her the nutrients she needs, and help her stay at a healthy weight for her age. Carrying extra weight puts more stress on joints in the hip, knees and ankles. On the other hand, if your child is too thin, she could benefit by gaining some weight.

The following tips may help your child increase her caloric intake during a flare, when she has little appetite:

- Prepare a variety of meals and foods. Ask what appeals to her, and try to make foods look "yummy."

- Concentrate calories by adding high-calorie items, such as butter and honey, to foods.

- Provide snacks that are good for her, such as nuts, fruits, granola bars or fruit juice.

- Encourage frequent meals or snacks.

- Make eating a pleasant event. Don't rush your child.

The effects of juvenile arthritis on a child's growth and development vary widely among individuals. A number of different factors are at play in this issue, including the type of juvenile arthritis, your child's age at diagnosis, the severity of disease activity, medications taken, and other issues. Because of the many variables involved, parents should have a frank discussion with their child's health-care team to determine what you might expect in your child's situation.

CALCIUM AND JUVENILE ARTHRITIS

Calcium is a necessary nutrient for the formation and normal strength of bones. Loss of calcium in bones is called osteoporosis. A bone with osteoporosis is weak and at greater risk for injury. The disease processes of juvenile arthritis and some of the medications used to treat it may put children at risk for developing calcium deficiency and osteoporosis. Therefore, children with arthritis, particularly those receiving glucocorticoids or methotrexate, are in need of adequate amounts of calcium to assure strength and growth of bones.

Recommendations for Children

Children 1-3 years of age
should receive 500 mg of calcium per day.

Children 4-8 years of age
should receive 800 mg of calcium per day.

Children and young adults 8-18 years of age
should have 1200 mg of calcium per day.

Calcium can be obtained either through diet, by calcium supplements, or a combination of both. Here are some dietary guidelines to help determine the amount of calcium in common foods.

8 oz. of whole milk = 291 mg
1 oz. of American cheese = 174 mg
1 cup of ice cream = 151 mg
8 oz. container of low-fat vanilla yogurt = 389 mg
Cocoa made with milk = 298 mg

If your child is not receiving the required amount of calcium from her diet, over-the-counter calcium supplements can help. Be sure to ask your doctor before putting your child on calcium supplements. These supplements are best absorbed when taken with meals.

Vitamin D is also important for children with juvenile arthritis because the body needs it to use calcium and for normal growth and development. Children can obtain adequate amounts of vitamin D along with their calcium when they drink three 8 oz. glasses of milk per day. Some brands of orange juice are also enriched with calcium and vitamin D. You can give your child one multiple vitamin tablet to provide the adequate amount of vitamin D if she is not getting enough in her diet. Excessive amounts of vitamin D can be harmful. Follow American Dietetic Association recommendations. Your child needs 400 IU (international units) of vitamin D daily.

Eye Care

Some children with juvenile arthritis develop an eye inflammation called iridocyclitis. Other terms for this condition include iritis and uveitis. Iridocyclitis may occur in JRA, most commonly in young girls with pauciarticular JRA who have a positive antinuclear antibody test (ANA blood test). This inflammation of the eyes may occur without obvious symptoms, but if left untreated it can cause blindness. Therefore, it is important for a child with any type of arthritis to have her eyes checked by an ophthalmologist as soon as she is diagnosed and regularly thereafter. This will ensure that any eye problems are detected early and treated, significantly reducing the risk of serious eye complications.

The ophthalmologist will give your child a complete eye exam, usually including a slit lamp test. This simple and painless procedure can spot problems long before symptoms are present. Your child should have periodic eye exams, because eye inflammation may occur even when the joint disease is inactive. The frequency of eye exams will depend on your child's risk for developing eye problems, which is determined by age, type of arthritis and presence or absence of antinuclear antibodies. If your child is diagnosed with inflammation in the eye, medicated eye drops will be prescribed.

Dental Care

The joint in front of the ears, where the lower jaw connects to the base of the skull, is the temporomandibular joint (TMJ). Arthritis may affect this joint in the same way it does other joints, resulting in pain, stiffness, swelling and altered growth. Jaw exercises and therapy may be recommended for the pain and stiffness. Medications can also affect your child's oral health and development.

Children with arthritis may have limitation of joint movement in the jaw, which can make brushing and flossing difficult. Your child's dentist may suggest various toothbrush handles, electric toothbrushes, floss holders, toothpicks and rinses that will help your child maintain healthy teeth and gums.

When the lower jaw does not grow properly, the child may develop an overbite. Your child's dentist may recommend an early consultation with an orthodontist if this occurs.

A child with active arthritis may not always have the stamina for even routine dental work. Shorter dental appointments may be helpful.

Summary

The more daily activities your child can do on her own, the healthier and happier she is likely to be. Encourage your child to remain physically active, but to use joint protection techniques in carrying out her daily activities. Your child should also eat a balanced, nutritious diet to be as healthy as she can be and to maintain proper body weight.

part three
LIVING WELL WITH JUVENILE ARTHRITIS

At first, the diagnosis of arthritis in a member of the family, especially in a child, can be upsetting to everyone. "What will this mean? How could this happen? What have we done to deserve this punishment? What will this do to the family?" These are all common questions that everyone wants answered. Many parents try to deny the truth. Some feel guilty. Eventually, though, most family members arrive at acceptance. At some point, everyone realizes that life must go on.

Though coping is hard and the extra problems may at times seem overwhelming, eventually a family makes a series of adjustments. Many families have found that the values of love, caring and sharing can be continued — and often made stronger — in a home with a child who has arthritis.

Following the
Medical Treatment Program

Children with arthritis can have difficulty following a treatment program. No one – particularly a child – likes to take medications, do special exercises or wear splints. However, following a treatment program consistently is more beneficial to your child and generally will make her feel better. In addition, this consistency will help the doctor or therapist to better evaluate the effectiveness of the treatment.

Because you, as a parent, are ultimately responsible for making sure your child follows prescribed treatments, you are an important part of the medical treatment team. This chapter provides specific suggestions about ways to help your child be more consistent in taking medications, doing exercises, wearing splints and complying with other prescribed activities. Feel free to use and adapt strategies that work for your unique family situation.

It's important that you and your child fully know how to perform a prescribed treatment and that you understand its purpose. At each doctor's office or clinic visit make sure you understand specifically what your child is to do, particularly if the doctor or therapist is adjusting the treatment plan to meet your child's changing needs. Refer to the section in Chapter 2 titled "How to Get the Most from Your Child's

Medical Visits" (page 16) for advice on making sure you understand and remember the doctor's instructions.

Helping Your Child Stick to the Plan

Reminders

One reason children don't follow prescribed treatment programs is that they simply forget. The following cues or reminders will help your child remember to do what is asked of her:

- Schedule treatments at the same time each day. Make sure that chosen treatment times blend in with normal routines and are convenient for your family. For example, exercises for younger children can be done during the late afternoon while they are watching favorite TV programs.

- Use an exercise video for children with arthritis. (See Resources on page 181 for more information.)

- Use a digital alarm watch set for times when your child has to take medications or do other prescribed activities. These watches are relatively inexpensive and can be reset each time your child completes part of her regimen.

- Use a chart or calendar to keep track of what your child should be doing on a daily basis.

Minimizing Negative Side Effects

Some children fail to do what's prescribed because the treatment causes problems or is uncomfortable. For example, range-of-motion exercises can be painful at times and some medications cause stomach pain. Reducing these negative side effects will help your child follow her treatment program.

- Warm the joints before exercising by soaking them in warm water or applying another heat treatment. (See Chapter 5 for more information on heat treatments.) This can make exercising less painful.

- Ask your doctor about ways to minimize stomach irritation caused by some medications. Many medications should be taken with food to avoid nausea.

Monitor Adherence

When your child has a chronic disease, it's important to monitor how well she adheres to treatment. This is true even for older children. Teenagers also need parental supervision to help them be consistent. By using the form on page 102, you can gauge your child's progress without badgering.

Post this form on the refrigerator. Each time your child takes medicine, does exercises or performs other prescribed activities, check it off let the child check it off or give her a sticker to put in the box. In addition, this method can remind children to perform other activities such as household chores.

Everyone needs encouragement, particularly children living with a sometimes frustrating chronic disease. When your child is consistently following the treatment program, reward her with positive feedback.

- Provide praise immediately after your child does what is asked of her. This is when it's most effective.

- Give positive feedback to both young children and adolescents. Teenagers like to hear positive comments, too (even though they may not admit it).

- Administer positive feedback in tangible ways. For example, allow your child to earn "tokens" (stickers, poker chips, etc.) for complying with her treatment program. These tokens can be cashed in for special activities, privileges or a weekly allowance.

Rewarding your child for following her treatment program is not bribery. You may believe your child should do what is requested because it can help her. However, children don't usually see the long-range consequences of their actions or their lack of action. A little positive reinforcement can provide a lot of motivation.

Don't Overreact

Your child's occasional complaining, whining and crying can be trying. However, if effectively handled, complaints are usually followed closely by cooperation and will diminish over time. If you are firm but don't lose your temper, most children will do what they are asked to (with a few complaints sandwiched in) and the incident will be over.

- Be sympathetic, but firm. For example, if your child starts to complain when asked to do her exercises, say, "I know you don't like to do the exercises, but they're helping you."

- If the complaining continues, ignore it, as long as your child continues to do what is asked of her.

- Don't fall into the trap of debating and arguing with your child. A lengthy debate with your child can grow into a full blown conflict.

- Ignore minor complaints and praise your child when she follows her regimen. Any reduction in the amount or volume of complaining is an improvement and should be rewarded.

- Tell older children you don't want to argue and walk away. Give your child a chance to comply with your request on her own.

Discipline

In spite of your best efforts to reward cooperation and ignore minor complaints, children occasionally refuse to cooperate. When this happens, you have few options but to discipline your child. Such disciplining is often difficult for parents – particularly for parents of children with chronic diseases. However, the best thing a parent can do for a child with a chronic illness is to treat her like any other child.

Discipline is not a synonym for punishment. It means setting rules and enforcing them in a way that best helps the child learn how you want her to behave. Pleading with, yelling at or spanking children is not likely to be effective; it's better to use methods that convey resolution and determination rather than anger or frustration.

Set limits for your children and make sure they know and understand these limits. Remember, children really do want boundaries to define their lives, although they test the boundaries often and from an early age.

The most effective discipline is administered in a firm but loving way. Be matter-of-fact and avoid arguing or yelling.

Summary

Helping your child follow her treatment program is a cooperative effort. You can help by being informed about the purpose of treatment, monitoring behavior, rewarding adherence and disciplining when necessary. Although it can be difficult to be consistent, particularly when positive results don't immediately occur, you can do much to help your child get the most out of her treatment program.

TREATMENT REGIMEN CHART

Name:_____ Date:_____

	Sun	Mon	Tues	Wed	Thurs	Fri	Sat
Medications							
Exercise							
Splints							

Emotional and Social Adjustment

Staying in the Mainstream

After the initial period of upheaval in adjusting to a diagnosis of arthritis, families begin learning how to incorporate arthritis into their lives without letting it run their lives. It takes flexibility, patience and the willingness to deal with uncertainty. In this chapter, we'll address the different ways arthritis can affect your family and provide strategies for coping.

Uncertainty and "Rain Check" Planning

Uncertainty is one of the first issues families of children with arthritis or any chronic illness must face. It is also one that can be the most frustrating. Because the disease has its ups and downs, a child may have periods of feeling fine and periods of not feeling well. Your child and the entire family will have to learn how to deal with some uncertainty.

The first step toward coping with uncertainty is to accept it as part of what comes with arthritis. Learn to plan ahead and to make allowances for changes that may have to be made.

Try having several types of family activities in mind as back-up plans – more active ones for good days; quiet ones for bad days. If you schedule a weekend outing, make back-up plans in case your child isn't feeling well enough to go. Perhaps a relative or babysitter can be on call to stay with the child if necessary. You can have some fun at-home activities ready (making cookies, watching a favorite video) so the child won't feel left out. Or, maybe you can simply wait a few hours until she feels better. This type of back-up planning is important for the whole family. Everyone needs to know that family members can still make plans and have fun, even if one family member isn't feeling well.

Your child can also learn to create alternative plans, so the uncertainty of the disease doesn't disrupt her activities. For example, when she and a friend plan an event together for a certain day, perhaps they could set a back-up date at the same time. If they decide to go shopping together on Saturday, and she feels too stiff or hurts too much to go, they can go the next Saturday, or the friend might come over for a quiet afternoon of games and movies instead.

If your family becomes used to scheduling choices and options when making plans, there will be fewer letdowns. Think in terms of a "rain check" in case the event needs to be held at another date.

Encourage a Positive Self-Image

As early as age three, a child with arthritis may realize that there is something different about her. This will affect her self-image, or the way she sees herself. The child may be aware, for example, that she can't play as vigorously as others. To help promote a positive rather than a negative self-image, try to emphasize what she can do, rather than what she can't do. Maybe she isn't a fast runner, but she may be a good swimmer, for instance. If she is not able to play on an athletic team, perhaps she can serve as manager or scorekeeper; or maybe she can get involved in a non-athletic hobby.

Treat your child as a valued, needed, contributing member of the family. Stress the uniqueness of every child. With consistent encouragement, she will develop self-confidence, independence and the ability to cope. Studies have shown that family chores and responsibilities play a significant role in the positive outcome of children. You may need to plan creative ways for your child to participate in family chores, but by all means make sure she has some duties of her own. Some examples of tasks that a child with arthritis can usually handle are feeding the pets, filling the salt shakers, setting the table, dusting, folding laundry, helping plan a vacation and making out the shopping list.

To help make sure that your child grows up feeling capable and productive, don't pity or overprotect her. Don't focus too much attention on small aches and pains. Certainly it's not easy to send your child off to school when she's in pain. However, keep in mind that helping her too much or not challenging her takes away from her sense of self-worth. Try to include her in everything, and expect a lot from her. One day when she's on her own, having to make all her own decisions, she'll thank you for treating her this way. Though it may be difficult to watch her struggle, don't help or permit other family members to help unless she really needs it. Praise her efforts, as well as her achievements. An occupational or physical therapist can offer more ways to help your child become independent.

Dealing with Feelings

Having a child with a chronic illness can be frustrating, stressful and exhausting. Feelings of guilt, embarrassment or despair may arise. It may take years to work through these feelings – but most families do in time. Remember that each family member, particularly the child with arthritis, will develop strength and rewarding qualities from meeting the daily challenges of living with arthritis.

Learning effective ways to manage stress can be a big help. To begin, try to separate the problems you can do something about from those you can't. Next, work on solving the problems you think you can solve. Then try not to worry further about the problems over which you have no control. Lastly, overcome the negative effects of stress. For instance, when frustration or anxiety makes you feel as if you could explode, let off steam in a positive way. Talk to a friend; take a walk; cry for a while – it's okay; pound some pillows; listen to music. Staying physically active can help reduce your stress level. Relaxation techniques are a great way to overcome the negative effects of stress. These methods relax your body and mind in a short period of time. Ask a counselor or therapist to teach you a few; also see the ones on page 69.

Remember Brothers and Sisters

The brothers and sisters of a child with arthritis need love and attention also; don't overlook them. Encourage them to share the responsibility of helping their sister or brother who has arthritis. They deserve honest, simple explanations about their sister or brother's illness. Don't be afraid to show emotion in front of them. That lets them know it's all right to feel sad, gloomy or even angry about their sibling's arthritis. Make sure your other children know that neither they nor you are responsible for your child's arthritis.

Don't forget about their important childhood experiences. Encourage them to have birthday parties or to have friends over to spend the night. Once in a while, do something fun with just one of the other children. Take turns. You might decide to go to a movie, the zoo or to share an ice cream cone at a corner store. Try to let your other children know that they are just as important and just as loved as their sister or brother with arthritis.

WHAT SIBLINGS ARE THINKING

A sibling's perspective of the child with arthritis and the disease will change as he ages. Following are some concerns parents might hear at various ages.

Elementary School and Younger

Did I cause the arthritis? Many children think they caused the arthritis by either hitting or kicking their brother or sister or wishing they would go away. Reassure them that they aren't responsible for the illness.

Can I get arthritis? It's common for children this age to think the disease might be contagious. The sibling might avoid contact with his brother or sister, and friends might not come over to play for fear of getting arthritis.

Middle School and High School

It embarrasses me when . . . Kids this age think standing out is the worse thing in the world. When children reach adolescence, everyone wants to be alike. Having a sibling who's different may be embarrassing to the child who doesn't have arthritis.

You mean this may never go away? Children often do not fully understand the meaning of the word "chronic" until they are 13 or 14 years old. When a child reaches this age, parents may have to explain the disease all over again. Siblings may think that after a certain point, life is going to return to the way it once was. It is hard for them to realize it won't.

The Impact on Your Marriage

The impact of a child with arthritis on a marriage can be dramatic. If you as parents relied heavily on each other for support in the past, you'll need it more than ever now. This will be a test of the strength of your relationship.

Suddenly you may feel that so many demands are being made on you, there isn't time or energy for each other. You may become depressed and, at times, short tempered.

Many times, the greater burden for taking care of the child's arthritis falls on the mother. It is usually better for everyone if the mother and father can share the duties. Dividing chores, such as assisting with your child's exercise routine, or taking her to medical appointments, reassures your child that both parents care about her. It also gives Mom a break, and allows Dad to feel like he, too, has an important role.

Raising a child with arthritis can be easier if you realize that no one is perfect! A very valuable way for you to deal with your feelings is to first accept yourself as a human being. Granted, you may not always encourage your child in the "right" way. Maybe sometimes you just don't have the energy to spend enough time with your other children or your spouse. However, have the courage to forgive yourself and go on.

Try to take some time just for your spouse. Originally, there were just the two of you, and after your children leave home, you'll be alone together again. Your relationship needs tending – a strong relationship takes effort. Create some time together – a night out, a walk or just some time alone together after the children are in bed. The happier you are, the better for your child. Couples who manage to work through such stressful times can develop bonds of great depth and lasting strength.

Lastly, make some time for yourself. Encourage your spouse to do so as well. Check to see if some kind of respite care is available in your area. This refers to programs that provide a qualified sitter while you are away, at low or no cost. Be a little bit selfish! If you do, you will feel renewed. You will also feel better able to cope with those special problems that come with a child who has arthritis.

Family Communication

One of the keys to coping is good communication among family members; that is, relating well to each other. When family members talk freely with each other, everyone has a voice in decision-making. When they don't, some may feel neglected or unimportant. The following are tips for good communication.

- Talk "with" rather than "to" a person. This means having a conversation with a person and listening for his or her ideas, rather than telling the person what to do. Most people respond better when they are asked rather than told to do something.

- Use "I" instead of "you" statements. For example, say "I get upset when you do that," rather than, "You make me upset when you do that." This way, the person with whom you are talking will not feel blamed or threatened and is more likely to hear and process what you are saying.

- Be an active listener. This means trying to understand what a person is thinking and feeling, as well as what he or she is saying. Respond to what you hear, but also what you "sense" the person is feeling.

- Try setting a time on a regular basis for family meetings. These events can be a good way to get everyone talking, discussing problems and creating solutions. Most families prefer to do this every day at the dinner table, rather than at an actual "meeting."

Raising a Child with Arthritis on Your Own

Being a single parent and raising a child with arthritis can be a very tough job. A key to coping is knowing people with whom you can talk and trust for support. Caring family members, friends and neighbors can make a great difference. With their support, you and your child *can* manage. Here are a few tips to help single parents cope:

- Work at having a social life for yourself. Don't let your child and her arthritis force you to remain at home with no social life.

- Ask for help when you need it, and learn to accept it graciously.

- Join or start a parents' group through your local chapter of the Arthritis Foundation.

- Become a member of Parents Without Partners.

Parents' Groups

Parents' groups are an excellent way to help parents cope with the stress of having a child with arthritis. Most important, they help mothers and fathers realize that they're not alone. Getting to know other parents who face similar situations proves that it can be done.

These groups can provide mutual support, friendship, compassion, understanding and awareness; practical ways to solve problems; education; talks by medical experts and speakers from community agencies; advocacy (working to support the rights of children with arthritis); and help with school services.

Call the nearest Arthritis Foundation office or the American Juvenile Arthritis Organization (AJAO) for more information (see listing under "Resources"). AJAO is a member component of the Arthritis Foundation that provides information, inspiration and advocacy to patients, parents, friends, relatives, health professionals and others interested in children with arthritis.

More Help for Families

Retreats, family conferences and weekend vacations shared by families of chronically ill children and health professionals are a growing resource for families struggling to cope. Through workshops, therapy sessions and recreational activities, families learn to express feelings, decrease stress and find resources for support.

For more information on finding a retreat in your area, contact your local university hospital, Arthritis Foundation office or the American Juvenile Arthritis Organization (AJAO) (See listing under "Resources"). The AJAO office can also provide information about their annual conference and other services for families and children with arthritis.

Finding Good Child Care

Perhaps you are a single parent, or perhaps both parents in your family need or choose to work. Even if one parent is able to be at home with the children, at times you will want and need to be away from your daily child-care activities. Because your child has arthritis, you want to choose child care even more carefully than most parents. The following suggestions may help you:

- Check to see who is available in your own neighborhood. Look for mature adult women who care for children or for other mothers with children who are about your children's ages. (Respite care, which can provide qualified sitters, could also be helpful.)

- Contact students in nursing or child development at local colleges or universities.

- Check with local child care facilities to see if they are staffed to care for your child.

- Form a neighborhood babysitting club.

Vacation Tips

Vacations are a great way to reduce stress, have fun together and become closer as a family. Your child's arthritis shouldn't hamper your vacation plans. A little advance planning and problem-solving can ensure a wonderful trip – and perhaps provide new opportunities for your child to face challenges and learn from them. The following tips should help make your family vacation a success:

- Ask the doctor to recommend another doctor who practices near your vacation spot.

- Know where health-care facilities are located.

- Bring a summary of your child's medical history and her treatment plan with you in case you need it.

- If you're driving, take breaks often to stretch or walk. This helps everyone stay relaxed.

- Bring your child's medication, splints and anything else that might be needed, such as a hot water bottle. Remember, encourage her to do her exercises and relaxation activities, and to remember joint protection and other important elements of self-care.

- If you need help when you are traveling by plane, call ahead to make arrangements with the airline.

- If your child has difficulty with stairs, request a ground floor room in your hotel or motel. Many facilities have special handicap accessible units that are equipped with bath stools, raised toilets or grab bars.

- Don't forget that a heated swimming pool can be great for exercising – for the whole family.

- Have fun!

Summary

A diagnosis of arthritis in one family member affects the whole family. At times the problems can seem overwhelming, but eventually a family makes a series of adjustments and learns how to go on with their lives. One of the most important keys to coping is good communication among family members.

Growing Up with Arthritis

Growing up isn't easy, and having arthritis can make the process more challenging. But everyone has challenges and obstacles in life; some are just more visible than others. Try to view your child's arthritis as just one more fact of life. Your attitude will help shape how your family adapts to the illness, how your child views herself and how well (or poorly) she copes with it now and as an adult.

Every day your child is growing and maturing. One of your main goals should be to constantly help her move toward independence. If you take full responsibility for her treatment program, there will be no reason for her to accept responsibility. If you find yourself often cajoling or arguing with her about her treatment program, it may be time to transfer more of the responsibility to her. By teaching responsibility and good self-care habits at an early age, you will have begun the process toward an independent adulthood. As your child grows, your relationship with her will change. The following guidelines are offered to give you a general sense of what your child is experiencing and needing at various stages of her development. Knowing this may help you determine how much responsibility to give her. Remember, arthritis is just a part of your child's life. Don't let it overwhelm your lives.

The child's age at the onset of arthritis will play a role in how she feels about having arthritis. Babies and small children will not remember life without arthritis. However, when the onset of arthritis occurs in an older child, the child will experience grief over the loss of the ability to do certain activities.

Ages and Stages

Infancy

During infancy, a child learns to trust, usually through her relationship with her primary caregiver. If her needs for food and comfort are met, she will learn that the world is a safe place. Through movement, she explores her world. She begins to express her desires and show her satisfaction. She is totally dependent on her parents for her care.

Age 2 to 3

In the toddler years, a child is capable of learning some self-care, such as feeding, dressing and grooming. At around three years old, the child wants to do everything herself. She has developed a mind and will of her own.

She is becoming aware of her differences and similarities to other people. This is the stage in which your attitude about her arthritis begins to influence her. If you are calm and at ease, your child will be, too.

Being apart from parents can be very upsetting to a child. If your child needs a blood test, for example, she will be calmer and less fearful if you are with her. Children at this stage act out negative feelings. For example, your child may give her doll or stuffed animal "a shot" after she has had to undergo an uncomfortable experience. It's very important that the child understand why she had the experience – otherwise she may feel that it was some kind of punishment. Allow your child permission to vent her frustration in appropriate ways. Help her play doctor with a doll and explain to the doll why procedures are necessary.

Age 4 to 6

During the preschool years, a child learns to do such things as brushing her teeth and putting away her toys. She can often remember to take her medication, and may really try her best to wear her splints at night. She may not understand why, however. She seeks approval from her parents, and likes praise. She may begin to develop a poor self-image as she realizes she can't do everything other kids can do. Parents need to try to reassure her whenever possible.

Most children at this stage are fearful of bodily injury or loss of control. They appreciate knowing exactly what is going to happen to them. Saying "This shot may hurt a little, so it's okay to cry if you want to," is helpful to a child at this stage.

By the time they're ready to begin school, most children are familiar with their medication. They know it by name and what it looks like. It's a good idea for them to be as aware of their specific medication and dosage as their parents.

Age 7 to 11

During the years of middle childhood, the child learns a lot about the world, about herself and about arthritis. She knows from experience that if she doesn't take her medication with food or milk, she might get a stomach ache. The child is more interested in knowing the reason why something must be done a certain way. She can be trusted more to carry out certain duties, such as doing her exercises and taking her medication.

She also should be allowed to make decisions and to fully participate in family events, if possible. She needs to be encouraged to talk about her feelings. Meeting other children with arthritis can help her realize that she isn't the only one who is a little different.

Her arthritis and the medication used to treat it may have some effect on her physical growth during this stage and the next two stages. Depending on what joints are involved, certain bones may grow too quickly or too slowly. If large doses of steroid drugs (glucocorticoids) are given for a long period, they can delay or affect a child's normal physical growth. Talk with your physician about the possibility of this in your child's situation.

Age 12 to 15

The preteen and early teen years are marked by rapid physical changes and the child's search for identity. The time between childhood and adulthood is difficult for most children. For children with arthritis, it can be even more difficult. At a time when body image is very important, joint misalignments, altered growth or delayed sexual development can make a teenager with arthritis painfully concerned about being different from others.

From time to time, frustrations can build up so that she may try to ignore her feelings by developing an "I don't care" attitude. She may stop taking her medications and performing her exercises. She may act selfishly and try to manipulate others. This can be her way of trying to gain some control in her life. Parents and other family members can help her by listening to her frustrations. They can remind her of her best qualities and skills, encouraging her not to dwell on her shortcomings, but rather her advantages. Parents should be careful about lecturing or judging her. Keep in mind that she will outgrow this stage.

She is still attempting to fully understand her arthritis. She can handle most of her arthritis management on her own, though she often needs prodding from family members in order to follow her treatment plan.

She may choose to meet with her doctor and other health professionals by herself. As she assumes more responsibility, she should practice more fully in planning her care. She expects and deserves privacy.

Age 16 to 19

At adolescence, the teenager can make management decisions. She knows that if she decides to skip her exercises, she will regret it. By age 16, she should be able to manage her care entirely on her own. She is developing her own attitudes and ideals, and may find her own role models. Her independence is important, yet is somewhat frightening at the same time. Her friendships outside the family will become increasingly more important to her. By age 18-19, she will depend even more heavily on the close friendships with others that she has established. Learning to establish this sense of intimacy will in turn enable her to enrich her life – and eventually seek a partner.

Making Friends

Whatever her age, your child, like every child, needs friends. Friends help her learn about herself. Relationships encourage her independence from you, broaden horizons, and help prevent her from dwelling on differences caused by arthritis. Your child will feel better about herself when she has friends she likes and trusts.

You can encourage these valuable experiences by allowing your child to invite friends to her home. If possible, provide them with a place of their own, where they can talk, listen to music, watch TV or play games. If your child's friends can't visit, there's always the phone or the Internet to help keep in touch. Find out about pen pal programs available through AJAO.

Because your child has a health problem, and may have some stiffness or swollen joints, she may at times be the target of staring, name-calling or other forms of teasing. You can help her deal with these situations by reminding her that usually children who tease do so for attention. Keep in mind that raising your child with a solid base of love, encouragement and praise can help her have the personal strength to cope with such situations.

Your child may want to tell her schoolmates about her arthritis during science class. This kind of informative session can bring her arthritis "into the open" and help her peers accept individual differences. Your child's teacher could remind the students that many of them have special challenges, too, like allergies or poor eyesight. Many children have health problems – that's one of the things that makes everyone unique and special.

Another way to lessen your child's emotional reaction to teasing is to encourage her to talk with you about it, and not to keep her feelings bottled up. Developing a sense of humor can help, also. For instance, an older child may freely admit to classmates that she cannot wait for the day when she can throw her splints away forever, or when she can begin the day without stiffness. Encourage her to talk to the kids about it. Keep in mind that the attitudes and values she gets from you will make a big difference in the way she is able to cope. If she is confident and likes herself, she will probably cope better with teasing.

Finding and Evaluating Camps

For many children with chronic illness, a summer camp can provide valuable experiences and opportunities for friendship. Many day and overnight camps offer programs for children with health concerns. If you are interested in sending your child to camp, you will want to carefully choose one that best suits your child's needs. Before you enroll your child, find out the following information: who manages and staffs the camp; the camp's goals; what medical care is available; the staff members' training and previous experience working with children who have special health needs; and what the camp can do for your child.

There are camps available especially for children with arthritis. Contact your local Arthritis Foundation office for more information.

Sexuality

Sex and sexuality are important and complex issues for teenagers and young adults. A teenager with arthritis, just as other teenagers, may be wondering: Am I attractive? Will I find a special friend? She may also be dealing with questions like: When will my arthritis go away? Will I be able to have a family? Can I have a career? Help her by emphasizing that no one is perfect, even if his or her body appears to be. Point out that arthritis isn't the only thing special about her. Remind her that people fall in love more with someone's personality than with physical appearance or abilities. Challenge her to continue to develop her own abilities and skills that can be used to create a happy and rewarding life for herself.

Most of her concerns will be common teenage worries – so talk about dating and openly discuss sex. Remember that your attitude is important. If you are comfortable and confident about your sexuality, she can develop a positive, healthy image with which to identify. If you need help discussing sex with your child, ask a social worker, counselor or another health professional for advice. As all adolescents mature, they begin to accept themselves, despite their imperfections. A teenager with arthritis can, too.

Summary

Your attitude helps determine how your family adapts to arthritis, how your child views herself, and how well she copes with it now and as an adult. By teaching responsibility and good self-care habits at an early age, you will have begun the process toward an independent adulthood.

part four
PRACTICAL MATTERS OF LIVING

As your child grows and moves further from the cocoon of family, she'll need strategies for coping with arthritis outside your home and for educating those she comes in contact with — her teachers, friends, potential employers and others. Arthritis may figure into what she is able to do at school, which college she chooses and what she chooses to do for a living.

When your child is young, you will need to help her deal with many of the issues that come up at school — whether or not she can take part in physical education class; what accommodations need to be made for her; when and how her medication should be taken. More importantly, you will need to make sure her teachers know the unpredictable nature of arthritis and how it affects your child in particular.

As your child gets older and goes off to college, starts a job or gets married, it's likely she'll have absorbed the practical approach you've taken to problem solving and will use that knowledge and matter-of-factness in getting through her day-to-day challenges.

School Issues

Most children with arthritis can and should attend regular school. Having arthritis does not affect a child's ability to learn and think, although pain and fatigue may, at times, affect her ability to concentrate. When your child enters school for the first time, or starts a new school, make sure her teachers have a copy of the Arthritis Foundation's pamphlet, *When Your Student Has Arthritis*. Also make sure a school-based occupational therapist or physical therapist is aware of your child's condition so he can work directly to help your child fully access the school environment and remain as independent as possible.

At some point you may need to consider whether you should use the formal special education process or a less formal approach. The Individuals With Disabilities Education Act (PL 94-142) guarantees a systematic approach to providing services for children with special needs in the school setting. The fact that your child has juvenile arthritis does not make her automatically eligible for special education; however, the case can be made for it if arthritis interferes with your child's ability to benefit from her education. Should you decide your child would benefit from special education, you will be referred to your school's special education department for a formal review process. An Individualized

Education Plan (IEP) is the written result of your child's evaluation under PL-142. The IEP will describe specifically what special services will be provided for your child and will include an instructional plan stating what your child will accomplish in special education during the school year.

Educating the Teachers

When your child starts school, and perhaps each time she has new teachers, talk to them about her arthritis or write a letter explaining her medical condition. See the sample letter from the student on page 126. Some parents have found it helpful to ask a member of the health-care team to help explain the child's needs. Continued communication between you and the teachers will help to guarantee the best possible growing and learning experience for your child.

Getting to school in the morning can be a real chore because of morning stiffness. It takes some children a couple of hours to take a warm bath, dress, eat and feel well enough to go to school. This takes planning and an early bedtime to ensure she gets the proper amount of sleep.

Issues to Address

The following are important issues that you need to address with your child's teachers and other members of the school staff.

- Work with your child's teacher to nurture a positive attitude and a sense of "can do" independence in your child. If this sense of optimism is expressed, the child and other students will also think, feel and act accordingly.

- Have your doctor send a letter to the school staff, outlining your child's abilities and limitations, medication schedule, any necessary physical or occupational therapy she may need during school hours and any other special services she may need.

- Make the school nurse and teachers aware of how your child takes her medicine. It is required that the school nurse handle all medications. Students may not carry medications in school.

- Let the teachers know that they should expect good school results from your child. They shouldn't expect lower grades or lack of interest because of arthritis – arthritis doesn't affect the mind. However, pain and fatigue may affect her ability to concentrate.

- Be sure the teachers understand that sometimes your child may be late for school because of morning stiffness. Make special arrangements to have missed work made up.

- Provide information so teachers understand that your child may walk and move a little more slowly than other children. She may need extra time writing and changing classrooms. She may or may not be able to climb stairs.

- Educate students in her class about arthritis and how it affects her. Talk with your child about this subject, and see how she feels. The topic should come up naturally. Many children with arthritis have volunteered to do a report on arthritis for their classes. Sometimes a member of the health-care team can help. Being open about the subject gives the other students a chance to learn about arthritis. It also fosters respect for the child and can help reduce teasing.

- Ask teachers to allow your child to get up and move about frequently to prevent stiffness. For example, maybe she can help collect papers, or pass out materials. It helps if her activities don't disturb the class or draw attention to her different abilities. She may also require rest periods during the day.

- Encourage your child's teachers, especially physical education instructors, to talk to her doctor or therapist to understand any physical restrictions she may have. Unless advised otherwise by her doctor, your child should be included in all school activities, up to her limitations. Children should set their own limits in physical education class and do activities to their own tolerance level, which may vary from day to day.

- Encourage your child's school or classroom to observe Juvenile Arthritis Awareness Week, held during March of each year. The week-long awareness effort, sponsored by the American Juvenile

Arthritis Organization (AJAO), is designed to increase students' understanding of arthritis. A variety of programs, including age-specific lesson plans for teachers, is available through AJAO. Contact your local Arthritis Foundation office for more information.

Here are two other suggestions to help your child at school:

- Encourage her to use a tape recorder to take notes, and a computer for writing assignments.

- See that the school allows her to have all her classes on the ground floor, or that an elevator is available so she can avoid climbing stairs. For more information on your child's educational rights, see the Arthritis Foundation's publication, *Educational Rights for Children with Arthritis: A Manual for Parents.*

SAMPLE LETTER TO TEACHER

Dear Teacher and School Nurse:

I am a student with arthritis and I would like you to know more about me. There are a lot of other kids like me (approximately 285,000 in the United States) but it is possible that because we are spread out all over the 50 states, you may never have had a child with arthritis in your class before.

There are some important things about me that I want to share with you. Sometimes I really hurt even though there isn't anything wrong with me that you can see. So if I am quiet, it doesn't mean that I'm not interested in school. Mornings can be a problem because my joints can be stiff for the first few hours after I get up and sometimes by late afternoon I feel tired. A lot of the time I feel really good but when my arthritis becomes active, I usually feel pretty uncomfortable. I hope this will explain why I have "up" days and "down" days.

I want to be in school whenever I can because I know that it is important for my education. I also want to be involved in as many activities and parts of school as I can. Sometimes it might be necessary to work out some special arrangements for me. I can't always take part in the regular playground or physical education programs. Sometimes I have a problem if the distance to the cafeteria or between classes is long or if I have to stand in long lines. I may need to take medication during school time because that is a very important part of my treatment for arthritis. And once in a while I may need to leave school for a doctor or physical therapist appointment.

I hope you will have a meeting with me and my parents if you have any questions or concerns. My mom and dad will keep you informed if there are any major changes in my condition during the year that you should know about. The nurse at my doctor's office can also tell you more about my disease and answer questions for you.

I have the same needs for accomplishment and success as all kids. So I want you to have the same expectations for me that you do for all other children. I may take more time, but I can do the same things the other kids do if you will let me. If I can't finish my work in time, please let me take home my assignment to finish instead of excusing me on the grounds that I have arthritis.

Attached is a list of other challenges I may have and some ways to help me manage in school. I have checked some areas of concern that I currently have in school.

Thanks for letting me tell you a little about myself. If you have any other questions, please feel free to ask me or my parents. Thank you.

Your Student

School Needs Checklist

You and your child can work together on this checklist or, depending on her age, she may be able to answer the questions herself. It can give her teacher a good idea of your child's strengths and weaknesses.

Have your child place an

A = always
S = sometimes
N = never
NA = does not apply to me

in the box next to each statement to describe herself.

Getting Ready for School

___ I can get out of bed without any help and without holding on to anything.

___ It takes me less than 30 minutes to feel good after I get up in the morning.

___ I must take a bath or shower to loosen up in the morning.

___ I can go up and down the stairs when I first get out of bed.

___ I can fully dress myself and put my shoes and socks on quickly in the morning.

___ I have a lot of pain in the morning before I go to school.

___ I need to bring splints, crutches, a cane or a wheelchair to school to help me during the day.

___ I go to school later in the day than the other kids because of my arthritis.

___ I take medication for my arthritis before I go to school.

Getting to School

___ I can walk to school or the school bus stop without any difficulty or help.

___ Waiting for the school bus is easy.

___ I can get into the school bus without any difficulty.

___ I need my parents to drive me to school or I take special transportation provided by the school.

Activities at School

___ I may need help dressing or undressing at school.

___ I can go up and down the stairs quickly at school without any difficulty.

___ I can use the elevator at school by myself without any difficulty.

___ I need to get up and walk around in the classroom because of stiffness or pain.

___ I can carry my own lunch tray.

___ I can open my own milk carton.

___ I need to take my arthritis medication at school.

___ I get embarrassed when I have to go to the school nurse.

___ I can use the bathroom by myself at school without any difficulty.

___ I find it easy to carry my own books at school and to and from school.

___ I can write at school without any pain or stiffness.

___ I find it difficult to write quickly.

___ I need more time than the other kids to take exams or complete homework because of my arthritis.

___ I find it hard to hold my pen or pencil.

___ I find it hard to write on the chalkboard.

___ I find it hard to use scissors to cut.

___ It is hard to raise my hand in class because of my arthritis.

___ I find coloring difficult.

___ I find painting difficult.

___ I get so tired at school, I want to rest.

___ I'm afraid that some of the other kids will knock me over.

___ I get frustrated because I can't always keep up with the other kids.

___ I find it difficult relating to the other kids at school.

___ I would like the other kids in my classroom to know I have arthritis as long as they don't treat me differently.

___ I find it difficult putting on or taking off my gym clothes.

___ I find it hard participating in regular gym activities.

___ Playing outside in cold weather is a problem for me.

___ Playing in the sun is a problem for me.

___ I need to protect my hands from the cold.

___ I get physical therapy at school.

___ I get occupational therapy at school.

___ I take a rest period at school.

___ I get teased at school.

I find it difficult to:
___ run
___ jump
___ hop

__ skip
__ play soccer
__ play basketball
__ play volleyball
__ play contact sports
__ other _____

After School Activities

__ I need to take a nap or a rest period when I get home from school.

__ I can finish all of my homework every night without difficulty.

__ I can participate in after-school activities without difficulty.

__ I cannot get through the school day and must go home early.

The type of arthritis I have is:

__ pauciarticular juvenile rheumatoid arthritis
__ polyarticular juvenile rheumatoid arthritis
__ systemic juvenile rheumatoid arthritis (Still's disease)
__ dermatomyositis
__ scleroderma (systemic sclerosis)
__ hypermobility syndrome
__ systemic lupus erythematosus (SLE, lupus)
__ spondyloarthropathy
__ psoriatic arthritis
__ other _____

I developed arthritis in (year)_____, when I was _____years old.
I currently have an IEP (Individualized Education Plan) __ Yes __ No
I missed _____ days of school during the school year _____
    because of my arthritis.

Physical Activity at School

Some activities may be fine for one child but too intense for another. In general, the child should be encouraged to set her own limits on activity at school and to let teachers know when she isn't feeling well. It may help your child's physical education teachers for you to complete the Physical Education Activity Guide on the following pages and provide it to them as a reference.

PHYSICAL EDUCATION ACTIVITY GUIDE

Date:_____Birthdate:_____

Student:_____School Grade:_____

This student has juvenile arthritis and requires the following modifications in the physical education activity program. If you have any questions, please contact:

_____

TYPES OF MOVEMENT	OMIT	MILD*	MODERATE#	UNLIMITED
Bending				
Climbing				
Hanging				
Jumping				
Kicking				
Lifting				
Pulling				
Pushing				
Running				
Stretching				
Throwing				
Tumbling				
Twisting				

Remarks:_____

_____

_____

TYPES OF EXERCISE	OMIT	MILD*	MODERATE#	UNLIMITED
Abdominal				
Arm				
Breathing				
Foot				
Head				
Knee				
Leg				
Trunk				
Relaxation				

Remarks:_____

_____

_____

* Very little activity
# Half as much as the unlimited program

COMMON SCHOOL CONCERNS FOR STUDENTS WITH JUVENILE ARTHRITIS

DIFFICULTY	STRATEGIES
Difficulty climbing stairs or walking long distances	Request elevator permit

Schedule classes to decrease walking and climbing

Request extra time getting from class to class

Use a wheelchair if needed |
| **Inactivity, stiffness due to prolonged sitting** | Change position every 20 minutes

Sit at the side/back of room to allow walking around without disturbing class

Ask to be assigned jobs that permit walking (collect papers) |
| **Difficulty carrying books/cafeteria tray** | Keep two sets of books; one in appropriate class, one at home

Have a buddy to help carry books

Get a backpack/shoulder bag for books

Determine cafeteria assistance plan (helper, reserved seat, wheeled cart) |
| **Difficulty getting up from desk** | Request an easel top desk and/or a special chair |

Handwriting difficulty (slow, messy, painful)	Use "fat" pen/pencil, crayons
	Use a felt-tip pen
	Stretch hands every 10 minutes
	Use a tape recorder for note taking
	Photocopy classmate's notes
	Use a computer for reports
	Request an alternative to timed tests (oral test, extra time, computer)
	Educate teacher – messy writing may be unavoidable at times
Difficulty with shoulder movement/dressing	Wear loose-fitting clothing
	Wear clothes with *Velcro* closures
	Get adaptive equipment from occupational therapist
Difficulty reaching locker	Modify locker or request alternative storage place
	Use two lockers with keylocks instead of dials
Difficulty raising hand	Devise alternative signaling method

Summary

Although arthritis does not affect a child's ability to learn and think, it can have an impact at school. Providing the school staff with plenty of information about your child's arthritis and any special needs she may have will help ensure that her educational experience is successful. The sample letter and checklists in this chapter may help start that dialogue.

Your Child's Future

A Time of Transition

As a teenager in high school, your child faces the usual difficult decisions in planning for her future: decisions about education, about career, about social life, about the process of becoming independent of you, her parents. There's a word for this process: transition. Transition refers to the stages we go through as we pass from one phase of life to another. For everyone, leaving the world of childhood to enter the adult world is one of the most important transitions we make.

A teenager with arthritis may confront some questions in making this transition that other teens don't have to deal with: What college can best meet my needs, both academic and physical? Will arthritis affect my career choice? Can I handle the responsibility of being on my own? Teens who developed arthritis at a young age may have a maturity beyond their peers. However, teens who are adjusting to new onset face many transitions – adjusting to a chronic illness, as well as making the transition to adulthood.

Determining Career Interests

Preparation for work and career begins in junior high or high school. Experts say that the earlier a child begins, the better. For most people – with or without arthritis – deciding what to do for the rest of your life is not easy. Your child may not finally make up her mind until she is actually in college or working. But the earlier she can identify areas of interest, the better you and she will be able to plan for the kind of education or training she needs.

Here are some general guidelines you and your child can use to narrow her choice:

- Identify her personal interests and strengths.

- Find out about jobs and careers in which she could best use her skills.

- Consider how arthritis might affect her ability to do the job she's interested in and how the job could be modified to suit her.

Finding Your Child's Interests

What kind of person is your child? To find out, have your child think about the following issues:

- Personal goals and values. What would she like to achieve in her life and to be remembered for? Helping others, making things work better, succeeding in business, living a life of adventure and excitement, raising a family, a combination of these, or some other achievement?

- Special interests. Ask your child to consider subjects she enjoys in school, favorite hobbies or activities, things she thinks about a lot.

- Special skills. Help your child analyze her strengths. Are they literary, mathematical, technical, managerial, artistic, manual, sales, analytical, business, conceptual or something else? If arthritis limits your child in some ways, is she able to make up for it in other ways?

- Personal characteristics. What qualities best define your child? Leadership, the ability to be a team player, the desire to be independent, artistic or technical? Is she a person who approaches strangers easily, or is she more reserved? Is she better at thinking about the big picture, or is she more detail-oriented? Does she thrive on pressure, or does it make her nervous? Does she feel that her work will be the most important aspect of her life, or does she see work as just one of many other interests?

One way for your child to learn more about her skills and abilities is vocational assessment, which is a process for finding out her interests, skills, work habits and special needs and matching them to particular careers or job training programs. Informal assessments are based on observations of her teachers and others who know her well. Formal assessments usually are given by trained professionals using standard-ized tests and procedures. Your child's school guidance counselor can help arrange for her to take these tests and can often provide other valuable kinds of information and help.

But What About Arthritis?

You and your child are in the best position to know her abilities and lim-itations. It is important to be realistic—but not negative—about what your child can and cannot do. Don't allow her limitations to become a restric-tion. Even if she is not likely to be able to perform the job she dreams of, she may be able to prepare for a rewarding position in the same field.

For example, say she's interested in a law enforcement career. If she's not physically able to be the cop at the crime scene, she could be the dispatcher who sends him there, the fingerprint expert who nails the criminal, the lawyer who advises the police chief, the computer expert who tracks down hackers or the reporter who tells the world the story.

The Americans With Disabilities Act (ADA), signed into law in 1990, was landmark legislation for people with disabiltiies, granting civil rights protection to people with disabilities similar to that provided to individuals on the basis of race, sex, national origin and religion. It guarantees equal opportunity for individuals with disabilities in employment, public accomodations, transportation, state and local gov-ernment services and telecommunications.

Thanks to the ADA, employers cannot discriminate against an indi-vidual with a disabilitiy in hiring or promotion if the person is otherwise qualified for the job. In addition, employers must provide "reasonable accommodations" to people with disabilities – for instance, equipment modification or job restructuring.

Summer and Part-Time Jobs

Nothing looks as good on a resume as experience. Summer and part-time jobs are a great way to gain experience and try out careers your child may be interested in while she is still in school. Don't overlook volunteer opportunities that can offer the same training. Even if paying or volunteer jobs do not fit your child's true career goals, they still can help her gain confidence in her abilities, acquire useful skills and develop good work habits. A satisfied employer may be a valuable reference when your child starts searching for her first "real" job.

In addition to the usual jobs in your community, two federal programs can help your child. The Summer Aid Program provides summer employment for economically disadvantaged youths. The Stay-in-School Program provides federal employment to help students in high school or a postsecondary institution resume or continue their education. Students earn while working part time (full time in summer) in federal agencies. Contact your local State Employment Service Office for more information.

The College Route

Preparation for college begins in high school. It involves several steps:

- Preparing for and taking either the Scholastic Aptitude Test (SAT) or American College Testing Program's ACT Assessment test – or both

- Deciding which colleges or universities to apply to

- Making a final selection

Preparing for College Admission Tests

SAT and ACT scores are important because they are used by many college admissions officers, together with other factors, to measure academic achievement and help predict how well a person is likely to do in college.

The SAT is a multiple-choice test made up of verbal and mathematical sections. The ACT assessment measures skills in four major areas:

English, mathematics, reading and science reasoning. Your child may apply to take either test with special accommodations (arrangements) if she has a physical disability and an Individualized Education Plan (IEP) on file at her high school. (See page 124 for more information about IEPs.) She may require extra time to stretch and walk around or assistance in filling out the testing sheet.

Selecting a College

If college is in your child's future, she'll need to think about many things in making her decision. Her high school college counselor can be her greatest ally; be sure to utilize whatever resources he or she can provide. But, in the meantime, here are issues you and your child should consider:

General Issues

Program. If your child is interested in a particular field of study, she'll want a college with a strong and respected program in that specific area. If she is still undecided, she may prefer to attend a college that is strong across the board so that she can try out a number of possible concentrations. Before she selects a school with a strong graduate program for undergraduate study, make sure its graduate admission policies are not biased against its own undergrad students.

Another option may be a local community college. Typically offering associate degrees, these colleges are supported by taxpayers and usually charge relatively low fees for tuition. They offer a wide variety of programs, including vocational and occupational courses. Your child can use a community college as a stepping stone to enter a university later or to take job-specific courses leading to a certificate of achievement.

Distance. You and your child should discuss how near home she would like to be. If she has not had much experience in taking care of herself or managing her own finances, she may wish to be near home. Or she may want to seize the opportunity to strike out on her own.

Atmosphere. Think about the college's unique atmosphere – whether it is large or small, urban or rural, competitive or low-key, diverse in its student body and extracurricular activities or homogeneous.

Cost. You'll need to think about cost and financial aid. See page 146 for more information.

Special Issues Affecting Students with Arthritis

Your child's arthritis may cause her to tire easily or make it difficult for her to move around. These factors could affect her choice of college, because some schools are more accessible to people with disabilities than others. It is usually better to choose a school that already offers special services than to have to ask for them to be initiated.

Most schools have an office of disability services (called different names at different schools) and this should be one of the first contacts at colleges your child is considering. At schools that place a strong emphasis on being accessible to students with disabilities, these offices may be able to help your child in many ways. They can help with:

- Academic support, such as special notetaking, testing or classroom accommodations

- Physical support, such as accessible parking, transportation, housing or personal assistance

- Adapted recreation and athletics

- Career or vocational support

- Information about helpful community resources

Experts strongly recommend visiting the campus of the school your child plans to attend to make sure it is as accessible as advertised.

Physical Factors in Selecting a College

Enrollment. A large university may have more services in place for students with disabilities; a small one may be more flexible and personal.

Size and Geography. A very large campus, or one that is very hilly, may be hard to negotiate.

Transportation. Are the public transportation system and the college bus service accessible to people with disabilities? If your child drives, is convenient accessible parking available?

Medical Facilities. Is the campus near a medical center where your child can receive specialized arthritis care if needed? It is a good idea to send copies of your child's medical records to a doctor near the college she selects.

Climate. How will the climate of the area affect your child's arthritis?

Building Accessibility. Do the buildings your child will use most often have ramps, elevators and wide hallways? How much distance is there between classrooms?

Bathrooms. Are there accessible bathrooms in the dormitory and academic buildings?

Extracurricular Activities. Are athletic facilities, student programs, sororities and fraternities, and recreational opportunities accessible and open to people with disabilities?

Getting the Most from the College Experience
It's easy to suffer academic overload in college. Taking on too much could result in exhaustion or even bring on an arthritis flare. Following these steps could help make your child's life easier.

Preregistration. Some schools allow early registration or grant priority registration for students with disabilities. This enables your child to select classes at locations and times of the day that accommodate her needs, and avoids long waits in line.

Class Selection. Your child should allow some time during each day for rest. If classes are scheduled one after another, she should plan a break after the second one. She should also try to avoid scheduling classes back to back, especially if they are not in nearby classrooms. Scheduling classes later in the day is a good idea if morning stiffness is a problem.

Reduced Course Load. Encourage your child to take only as many courses as she can handle without an undue amount of stress. Remind her, though, that challenge is a part of college and she should not use her arthritis as a cop-out. If she does need to cut back, check in advance whether this could affect her financial aid and health insurance. Because her financial aid may require that she maintain a certain number of credit hours, you may need to make special arrangements for it to be continued. If she is carried on your health insurance as a dependent full-time student, she may risk being dropped if her course load falls beneath a minimum number of hours.

Communicating with Instructors. Talking with instructors or teaching assistants before classes begin is highly recommended. Your child should discuss with them how arthritis or sudden flares could affect her work or ability to complete some assignments or tests on time.

Special Accommodations. Your child may be allowed to use a note taker, tape recorder, lap-top computer, or other equipment if she has difficulty writing because of arthritis. Special seating can also be arranged.

Exam Modifications. Your child may request extended time for test taking, an afternoon test time, an oral instead of written exam, or other needed modifications.

Residential Issues in College

Choosing a place to live while at college is a very important decision. As a freshman, your child may be required to live in a dormitory on campus. Even so, she will have choices to make.

The most important aspect of choosing a place to live is to actually see what you are choosing. Be sure your child makes an appointment to see her room options and to test the room for her specific needs. Your child should make an appointment to go through her room and see what changes she may need. Some schools will make the changes for her.

Explore Attendant/Roommate Choices

For many new college students, independence is the most important aspect of going to college. But if your child has severe arthritis flares or very limited function, consider having an attendant or roommate help with things like laundry, shopping and cleaning. It might be a good idea to have an attendant to help out for the first quarter/semester of college, until your child becomes accustomed to the routine.

The person chosen as your child's attendant should be flexible. What he or she will be asked to do often depends on your child's energy and physical level. It is very important for your child to be honest with the attendant and to do what she can. On the other hand, your child's attendant must understand that this is a job and that your child depends on him or her.

Finding and Paying an Attendant

Start your search for an attendant early. Try the school's disabled student services office, local health agencies and ads in the school's student newspaper. The best option, however, may be an ad posted in the hall where your child will live while the previous year's students are still in the hall. Just showing up and asking floormates to help can lead to bad feelings.

Be very cautious about asking a good friend of your child's to be her attendant. In some cases, this can strengthen a friendship. However, since the attendant will be your child's employee, this can create a touchy situation between friends.

Payment will greatly increase the chances of attracting an attendant. Most schools' residential life programs offer some sort of compensation; some give attendants a free room. Some federal programs such as vocational rehabilitation also pay for attendant care.

Get to Know the Residence Advisor

Make sure your child contacts her residence advisor as soon as possible. Let him or her know what to do and whom to contact if your child has any special emergency needs. Your child should let her residence advisor know if she is having problems adjusting to dorm or college life. This person is also an excellent resource for becoming involved in campus activities, organizations and events.

Don't Be Afraid to Participate

Because accessible rooms, bathroom and shower facilities tend to be constructed differently, they may be a little out of the way of other rooms. Your child should not hide out in her room. With her residence advisor's assistance, your child should take part in programs and activities that are hosted by residence halls or individual floors.

Be Assertive

Encourage your child to be assertive. She should make it clear that she does not want to be treated differently. Her residence advisor can help her make this point, if needed. Her floor/hall is a community, and she has a right to be an equal member of it.

After a year or two, your child may think about living off-campus. A dorm provides housing, food, companionship and security, but it may be restrictive. On the other hand, the independence of living off-campus has to be balanced against the loss of these support services.

A Word to Party Animals

Getting "wasted" from time to time may seem cool to college students. People your child meets may pressure her to drink or try illegal drugs. She may be tempted to go along with them, either to fit in or because of pressure, loneliness or depression. However, as a person with arthritis, she should be very careful about drinking alcohol and using illegal drugs. You should help her understand that alcohol and drugs can produce dangerous reactions when combined with the medications she takes. She also risks falling and other accidents that could damage her joints.

Education Costs

By combining federal and non-federal loans, grants and scholarships, you may be able to put together a financial aid package that goes a long way toward covering the costs of your child's education. Because different schools offer different types of aid, you may be able to "shop around" to get the best deal. The college counselor at your child's school should be able to provide you with information and advice on applying for financial aid. Money shouldn't be your only criterion for selecting a school: overall educational quality and your child's career goals count too.

Vocational Rehabilitation Assistance

Your state Vocational Rehabilitation (VR) agency is an excellent source of information about financial aid and other kinds of help for students with disabilities. The help VR offers may include the following services:

Tuition Expense. Your child's VR counselor can direct you to sources of financial aid, including federal and state programs. If these do not cover your expenses and your child meets VR's eligibility requirements, the agency may also be able to provide tuition assistance to make up the difference. In many cases, the VR counselor will work with financial aid administrators at postsecondary schools to provide support.

Independent Living. A VR counselor may be able to help you with medical services, transportation and other assistive devices and personal assistance services that promote independent living.

Summary

Leaving the world of childhood and becoming an adult is one of the most important transitions we make in life. For a teenager with arthritis, this transition can be even more challenging – in addition to the usual responsibilities of adulthood, your young adult will need to take responsibility for managing her own day-to-day arthritis treatment. The choices your child makes about her life may also need to be influenced by her arthritis. You and your child are in the best position to know her abilities and limitations. It is important to be realistic – but not negative – about what your child can and cannot do.

Financial Issues

Personal Medical Insurance

The high cost of caring for a child with arthritis can be a constant source of stress for a family. If your employer offers choices of group insurance, choose the most comprehensive policy. Comprehensive means that almost every medical expense is paid for. Comprehensive major medical insurance usually covers hospital, surgical and medical expenses. Make sure that inpatient and outpatient (clinic) care is covered as well as physical therapy, occupational therapy and splints. Most of the time, these policies carry a deductible, which means you have to pay a certain amount each year before the insurance company pays the bill.

Health-care services have been dramatically reorganized under managed care in an attempt to produce efficiencies and cost savings. Managed care organizations attempt to control costs by developing special financial arrangements and coordinated provider networks offering a full range of services. Some health-care providers are under contract with certain health plans and are paid a set amount of money each month for each member of a plan, regardless of what services are provided.

The three main types of managed care plans include:

Health Maintenance Organizations (HMOs)

HMOs are prepaid, comprehensive medical plans. This means that the health-care plan has agreed to treat you for a certain set fee that's paid in advance to the HMO. In order to be covered for services, you must use the providers in the HMO network. Typically, patients must be evaluated by their primary doctors for referral to specialized care, such as a pediatric rheumatologist. Some HMOs don't require deductibles or co-payments.

Preferred Provider Organizations (PPO)

A PPO is a network of health-care providers and facilities that have agreed to treat participants for a specified negotiated fee for each service. As long as you choose a PPO provider in your network, most services will be covered in full, or close. If you use a provider outside the network, the PPO will pay 60 to 80 percent of the "reasonable and customary" fees (as defined by the PPO) and you must pay the rest.

Point of Service (POS) Plans

POS plans offer members the choice of receiving care through network providers or going outside the network to a provider of choice. If you go outside the network, you pay a much higher portion of the cost out of your pocket.

Traditional Health Plans

Other health plans are based on the traditional fee-for-service arrangements between the insurers and the providers. This means that the providers are paid per service they provide. Many of these plans now use managed care techniques to control costs.

Shop Wisely

If you need to supplement your group coverage with an individual policy, or if you don't have group coverage, shop around for the best individual policy. Study its rules, restrictions, exclusions and waiting periods. Check whether the policy has pre-existing condition limitations; often there is a waiting period before these will be covered. A Federal law has been passed mandating that states must prevent insurance companies from enforcing a waiting period on coverage of pre-existing conditions, as long as the person has been continuously covered by some type of health insurance.

Try to find a policy that will allow your child to continue being insured after she is no longer your dependent. As your needs change, and medical care costs continue to rise, you may need to "upgrade" your individual insurance policies. For example, if your insurance only pays $100 a day for a hospital room, and the going rate is many times that, you'll need more coverage.

Tips for Helping Meet Medical Expenses

- When completing income tax forms, take advantage of every possible medical deduction. Keep all bills, receipts (for parking, gas, medications, meals) and records in one safe place and save them as proof of your expenses. Ask the doctor to write prescriptions for certain items that your child needs. For example, medications, splints, wheelchairs, medical appliances, special clothing or mattresses can all be tax deductible if prescribed. Some of these prescribed items may be covered by your health insurance.

- Consult with the hospital's accounting department for help with insurance claims.

- Several possible sources of financial assistance may be available. Ask the social worker to help you identify which ones are suitable.

Federal Programs

Supplemental Security Income (SSI or Title XVI)

This program provides cash to people who are disabled and have limited incomes. The "disabling condition" must be expected to last at least 12 months. To be eligible, a child with arthritis usually has to have persistent joint inflammation and limitation of motion, fixed deformity and proof by x-ray of involvement of parts of the body other than the joints.

Social Security Disability Insurance (SSDI or Title II)

This is another program that provides money to disabled workers.
A child disabled by arthritis can receive benefits under this program if one of her parents who is covered by this program retires, becomes disabled or dies.

Medicare

This health insurance program protects certain severely disabled people regardless of age. It will award benefits to people who have been receiving SSDI benefits for at least two years.

For more information about any of these programs, contact your local Social Security office.

State Programs

Medicaid Supplemental Care Assistance

This program is designed to help cover costs of care of people with few financial resources. Eligibility requirements vary from state to state.

Children's Special Health-Care Services

Every state has a special services agency that can provide diagnostic and medical services for children under 21 who have disabling conditions. These services vary from state to state.

In 1997, Congress passed the Balanced Budget Act which requires that states develop programs for uninsured children; it is called Kids' Care Insurance.

Vocational Rehabilitation Services

Most states can provide some forms of financial aid through this agency to qualified youths with disabilities who are 16 and over . For example, some states assist with college tuition, self-help aids, typewriters, wheelchairs, a salary for an attendant and aids to enable teenagers to drive. See page 146 for more information.

Voluntary Groups

Jaycees, Shriners, Kiwanis, and many national social sororities and fraternities offer various paid medical services for children with arthritis.

Summary

Medical care for a child with arthritis can be a source of financial stress for a family. To minimize your expenses, shop wisely for health insurance, know the available tax deductions and educate yourself about any federal or state programs that may help.

14

Knowing and Protecting Your Child's Rights

Advocacy means speaking out on behalf of yourself or others to ensure access to needed services. Parents of children with arthritis across the country have advocated for access to a quality education and excellent medical care. Advocacy for children with arthritis can involve learning about laws and services, lobbying elected officials or writing to insurance companies regarding covered services. On both a local, grassroots level, and in collaboration across the country, parents can work together for change. Developing a relationship with elected officials through letter writing and phone calls can be powerful.

Thanks to the advocacy efforts of parents like yourselves, there are now pediatric rheumatology centers in every region of the country. Many of these centers were initially funded by the federal office of Maternal and Child Health under the Title V, Social Security Act. Located at major university medical centers, these centers are devoted to research, training, and the diagnosis and treatment of children with arthritis. In 1996, a National Institute of Arthritis, Musculoskeletal and Skin Diseases grant was awarded to Children's Hospital Medical Center at the University of Cincinnati to establish the first pediatric arthritis research center.

Your Child's Rights

Several federal laws define existing entitlements in education that many children with arthritis qualify for. However, the interpretation and the enforcement of these laws varies from state to state.

The following are federal laws that define specific services for children with disabilities:

- Rehabilitation Act of 1973, Section 504: Mandates equal opportunity to receive services from programs receiving federal funds (including schools).

- Education for All Handicapped Children Act of 1975: Mandates free, appropriate public education in the least restrictive environment with related services that allow the child to reach maximum potential.

- Education for All Handicapped Children Act, Amendment 1986: Mandates assessment of family needs and provision of multi-disciplinary services for preschool children with developmental delays or disabilities.

- Individuals with Disabilities Education Act (IDEA), Amendment 1990: Changed the name of the original act from Education for All Handicapped Children Act to IDEA, and broadens services for students with disabilities. More clearly defined "related services".

- Americans with Disabilities Act (ADA) of 1990: Protects individuals with disabilities from discrimination in employment. Mandates reasonable accommodations that permit these employees to perform their jobs. ADA requires private schools, day-care centers and nurseries to be accessible to children with disabilities. The ADA is a civil rights act with very broad applications. It does not specifically guarantee the right to a free appropriate public education, which is already guaranteed under IDEA.

- IDEA re-authorization 1997: Established "interim alternative educational setting" (IAES) to address serious discipline problems in students with disabilities. Expanded developmental delay definition to include ages 3-9.

Other laws that provide funds to pay for services for children with arthritis are:

- Head Start Act: Provides preschool children with educational training and health-care exams or treatment.

- Child Care and Development Block Grant: Mandates that states provide day care, transportation, treatment, recreation and counseling to children with developmental disabilities.

- Vocational Education Act: Mandates that states provide an individual vocational education plan.

- Maternal and Child Health Services Block Grant: Provides for medical, surgical and corrective services for children who are diagnosed with conditions that could lead to disability.

Specific Problems with Coverage and Services

Despite the existing federal mandates, many children with rheumatic diseases still do not have adequate access to all the social and special education services they and their families need. Compounding this problem is limited access to specialized pediatric rheumatology care. There are only about 350 pediatric rheumatologists in the United States, most of whom are located in metropolitan areas. In small cities and rural areas, children with arthritis are usually cared for by a general rheumatologist and/or a general practice pediatrician. Many children must travel periodically to see a pediatric rheumatologist, who then works with local physicians to coordinate appropriate care.

The inadequate number of full-service pediatric rheumatology centers creates a variety of problems for families. Children with rheumatic disease need services like physical therapy, occupational therapy, social work or vocational counseling -- services often available only in a large pediatric rheumatology center. Legally, though, your child has a right to obtain these services at school, thanks to the Individuals with Disabilities Education Act (IDEA). It guarantees all children the right to a free and appropriate public education. Under the legislation, eligible children can receive services from the school that are necessary to keep them functioning in school.

Unfortunately, many children who should receive these services in school don't. The determination of when a service meets an educational need and when it meets a medical need is often unclear. As a result, schools sometimes shift responsibility to the health care system, and the health care system may not understand the role of school services. In addition, the health care and school systems have historically had little coordination of services.

Parents must be the child's advocate to make sure their child obtains needed services in the midst of two often competing and uncoordinated systems. Knowing who to ask, how to ask, when to ask, and what to ask for will help you and your child succeed in getting the best quality of life in school and beyond. Persistence is the key when it come to affecting changes.

Power in Numbers: Advocating Together

If you are not already involved, you may want to join an American Juvenile Arthritis Organization (AJAO) parents' group at your local Arthritis Foundation chapter. Becoming a member of such a group can help you learn more about the laws and rights of children with arthritis and work collectively for change.

If you've never advocated for legislative change before, now is a perfect time to start. As the pressure increases to contain health-care costs, optimum care for children with arthritis may be further jeopardized. Misperceptions about both the severity of arthritis and the value of comprehensive treatments are a threat to the priority arthritis care may receive under cost-containment plans. AJAO supports the movement to control costs while maintaining access to quality care.

The Arthritis Foundation and AJAO work closely with other organizations and individuals to add strength and credibility to advocacy efforts. These include organizations such as the American College of Rheumatology, the American Nurses Association, the American Medical Association, the American Hospital Association and others.

Strategies for Improving Services for Children with Arthritis

Interpretation of federal laws regarding children with chronic disease varies widely from state to state. States provide reimbursement for evaluation, diagnosis and treatment for some children with special needs through Children's Medical Services (CMS) or Children With Special Health Care Needs, but eligibility requirements vary from state to state. In some states, children with juvenile rheumatoid arthritis are eligible to receive services, while children with other rheumatic diseases, such as lupus, are not. The family income level for eligibility also varies widely among the states. Finally, the actual services reimbursed are inconsistent. Some states also restrict the types of specialists families can see under this program.

The Arthritis Foundation promotes establishing a national standard of eligibility for the Children's Medical Services program that would include all childhood chronic diseases. The Foundation also supports expanding Medicaid to provide health insurance to all children, and the investigation of other options such as school-based health insurance programs.

Additionally, AJAO and its parent organization, the Arthritis Foundation, work actively to promote the following strategies:

- Encourage the creation of more pediatric rheumatology centers offering a full range of health-care services to children with rheumatic diseases.

- Advocate for expanded clinical and basic research in pediatric rheumatology.

- Build national coalitions to promote a standard definition of eligibility for, and responsibility for provision of, needed services in schools. Build state-level coalitions to push for the implementation of such standard definitions in states.

In addition to its advocacy efforts, AJAO provides information, support and advocacy training to families of children with arthritis; educates community physicians about pediatric rheumatology; develops materials to assist guidance counselors and school administrators in helping students receive vocational education services; and promotes public awareness of juvenile arthritis.

Summary

The Arthritis Foundation and the AJAO work actively to ensure that people with arthritis and other rheumatic diseases receive the care and services they need. We believe the goal of access to total care includes all the services necessary to preserve health, prevent loss of function and maintain the highest possible quality of life. It is largely through the collective advocacy efforts of thousands of parents that laws have been changed and continue to change.

In Conclusion

Your hope is to have your child and the rest of the family lead a happy and rewarding life. This book offers some ways to help you. Remember to keep a positive attitude, and encourage your child to be responsible for taking care of herself. Despite daily ups and downs, your family *is* coping with arthritis. Talking together, caring for each other, and working together as a family will allow you to successfully meet the daily challenges of arthritis.

Most importantly, keep your child in mind. Your natural tendency as a loving parent may be to help her too much, to do too much for her. But remember to encourage her independence whenever you can. Love her and support her, but learn to trust her and have faith in her. Remember she is a wonderful, unique individual who just happens to have arthritis.

Varni/Thompson Pediatric Pain Questionnaire
(Reprinted with the permission of James Varni, PhD)

Name _____

Age:_____

Date:_____

What words would you use to describe pain or hurt?

_____

_____

_____

From the words listed below, circle the ones that best describe the way it feels when you hurt or are in pain.

cutting	squeezing	stretching	sickening
beating	pulling	terrible	uncomfortable
burning	cruel	tiring	warm
scraping	sad	horrible	unbearable
pricking	aching	biting	flashing
pinching	cool	cold	jumping
stinging	pins & needles	miserable	scared
fearful	spreading	itching	sore
hot	deep	pressing	punishing
bad	stabbing	tight	lonely
sharp	screaming	tingling	
pounding	tugging	throbbing	

From the words you circled, which three words best describe the pain you are feeling right now?

Put a mark on the line that best shows how you feel now. If you have no pain or hurt, you would put a mark at the end of the line by the happy face. If you have some pain or hurt, you would put a mark near the middle of the line. If you have a whole lot of pain or hurt, you would put a mark by the sad face.

Not Hurting
No Discomfort
No Pain

Hurting a Whole Lot
Very Uncomfortable
Severe Pain

Put a mark on the line that best shows what was the worst pain you had this week. If you had no pain or hurt this week, you would put a mark at the end of the line by the happy face. If the pain or hurt you had was some hurting, you would put a mark by the middle of the line. If the worst pain you had was a whole lot of pain or hurt, you would put a mark by the sad face.

Not Hurting
No Discomfort
No Pain

Hurting a Whole Lot
Very Uncomfortable
Severe Pain

Body Outline for Pain

Place on a table eight basic color crayons. Ask your child to choose colors to represent No Pain, A Little Pain, More Pain, and A Lot of Pain to you and color in the boxes. Now, using those colors, color in the body to show how you feel. Where you have no pain, use the No Pain color to color in that body part. If you have hurt or pain, use the color that tells how much pain you have.

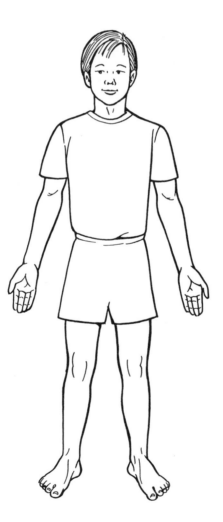

No Pain   A Little Pain   More Pain   A Lot of Pain

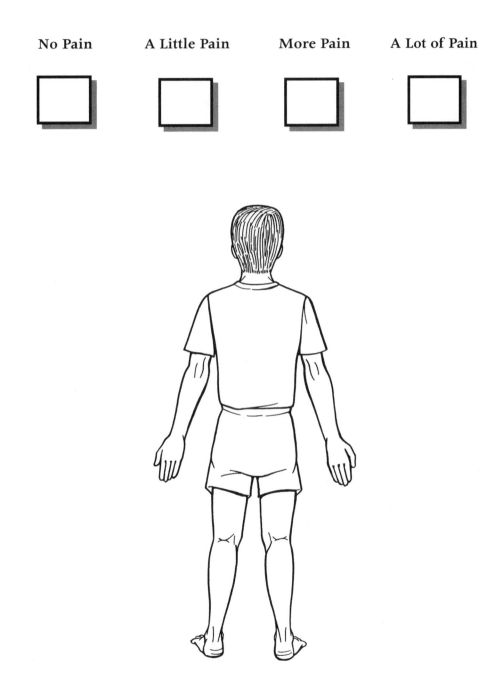

The majority of children with chronic arthritis have one of the forms of juvenile rheumatoid arthritis: polyarticular, pauciarticular or systemic JRA. However, there are over a hundred different forms of arthritis and related conditions that can affect children. Many of these conditions are rare, and specific information about some forms of arthritis and related conditions can be difficult to obtain. Therefore, the following classification list is included to help clarify how the different types of arthritis and related conditions are currently divided into categories and to facilitate communication about these conditions.

Classification of Rheumatic Diseases in Childhood

(Reprinted with permission from *Textbook of Pediatric Rheumatology*, Third Edition by James T. Cassidy, MD and Ross E. Petty, MD, PhD)

Inflammatory Rheumatic Diseases of Childhood
  Chronic Arthropathies
    Juvenile Rheumatoid Arthritis (JRA)
      Pauciarticular JRA (4 joints or less)
      Polyarticular JRA (5 joints or more)
      Systemic JRA
    Spondyloarthropathies
      Juvenile-onset ankylosing spondylitis
      Juvenile-onset psoriatic arthritides
      Arthritides with inflammatory bowel disease
      Reiter's syndrome
    Arthritis associated with Infectious Agents
      Infectious arthritis
        Bacterial
        Spirochetal (Lyme disease)
        Viral
        Other
      Reactive arthritis
        Acute rheumatic fever
        Post-enteric infection
        Post-genitourinary infection
        Other

Connective Tissue Disorders
  Systemic lupus erythematosus
  Juvenile dermatomyositis
  The sclerodermas
    Systemic sclerosis
    Localized sclerodermas
    Mixed connective tissue disease (MCTD)
    Eosinophilic fasciitis
    Other
  Vasculitis
    Polyarteritis
      • Polyarteritis nodosa
      • Kawasaki disease
      • Microscopic polyarteritis nodosa
      • Other
    Leukocytoclastic vasculitis
      • Henöch-Schönlein purpura (HSP)
      • Hypersensitivity vasculitis
      • Other
    Granulomatous vasculitis
      • Allergic granulomatosis
      • Wegener's granulomatosis
      • Other
    Giant cell arteritis
      • Takayasu's arteritis
      • Temporal arteritis
    Other

Arthritis and Connective Tissue Diseases Associated with Immunodeficiencies
  Complement component deficiencies
  Antibody deficiency syndromes
  Cell-mediated deficiencies

Noninflammatory Disorders
  Benign Hypermobility Syndromes
    Generalized
    Localized

  Pain Amplification Syndromes and Related Disorders
    Growing pains
    Primary fibromyalgia syndrome

Reflex sympathetic dystrophy (RSD)
Acute transient osteoporosis
Erythromelalgia

Overuse Syndromes
Chrondromalacia patellae
Plica syndromes
Stress fractures
Shin splints
Tennis elbow, Little Leaguer's elbow, tenosynovitis

Trauma
Osteochondritis dissecans
Traumatic arthritis, non-accidental trauma
Congenital indifference to pain
Frostbite arthropathy

Pain Syndromes Affecting Back, Chest or Neck
Spondylolysis and spondylolisthesis
Intervertebral disc herniation
Slipping rib
Costochondritis
Torticollis
Aneuralgic amyotrophy

Skeletal Dysplasias
Osteochondrodysplasias
Generalized
Achondroplasia
Diastrophic dwarfism
Metatrophic dwarfism
Epiphyseal dysplasias
Spondyloepiphyseal dysplasias
Multiple epiphyseal dysplasias
Osteochondroses
Legg-Calvé-Perthes disease
Osgood-Schlatter disease
Thiemann's disease, Köhler's disease
Freiberg's infraction
Scheuermann's disease

Heritable Disorders of Connective Tissue
Osteogenesis imperfecta
Ehlers-Danlos syndrome
Cutis laxa
Pseudoxanthoma elasticum
Marfan's syndrome

Storage Diseases
Mucopolysaccharidoses
Mucolipidoses
Sphingolipidoses

Metabolic Disorders
Osteoporosis
Rickets
Scurvy
Hypervitaminosis A
Gout
Ochronosis
Kashin-Beck disease
Mseleni disease
Fluorosis
Amyloidosis

Systemic Diseases with Musculoskeletal Manifestations
Hemoglobinopathies
Hemophilia
Diabetes mellitus
Hyperlipoproteinemias
Pseudohypoparathyroidism
Secondary hypertrophic osteoarthropathy
Sarcoidosis

Hyperostosis
Infantile cortical hyperostosis (Caffey's disease)
Other

acetylated salicylates: A family of medications such as aspirin that help relieve headaches, mild pain and fever. They are part of the nonsteroidal anti-inflammatory group of drugs.

acute: Having a short and relatively severe course.

anaphylaxis: Extreme sensitivity to certain medications or other substances, often resulting in shock and life-threatening respiratory distress; allergic shock.

anemia: A condition in which the red blood cell count is too low.

anesthesiologist: A medical doctor who uses drugs (anesthesia) to make certain a person is asleep and cannot feel pain during surgery.

anesthetist: A nurse who administers anesthesia during surgery.

ankylosing spondylitis: A type of arthritis involving inflammation in the spine that can cause the joints to fuse, or grow together. In children, the disease generally causes arthritis in the large joints of the lower extremities, such as the hips.

anterior: Situated in front of or in the forward part of an organ.

antinuclear antibody (ANA) test: A blood test to determine whether certain antibodies that indicate an autoimmune illness are present.

arthralgia: Pain in a joint.

arthritis: Literally means joint inflammation (arth = joint; itis = inflammation). It generally means inflammation of a joint from any cause, such as infection, trauma or an autoimmune disorder.

arthroscopic surgery: Surgery done inside a joint, using a thin tube with a light at the end, which is inserted through a small incision. This type of surgery is best for minor repairs, such as removing torn or loose cartilage.

autoimmune disorder: A malfunction of the body's immune system in which the body appears to attack and damage its own tissues. There are many types of autoimmune disorders, including arthritis and related conditions.

calcinosis: A condition in which calcium salts are deposited in various tissues of the body. Also called calcium gout.

cardiologist: A physician who specializes in the diagnosis and treatment of heart diseases.

chronic: Long-lasting or persistent.

contractures: A joint deformity caused by loss of motion and shortening of the surrounding tissues.

Cushing's syndrome: A possible side effect of taking glucocorticoid medications; symptoms include weight gain, moonface, thin skin, muscle weakness and brittle bones.

dietitian: A specialist in nutrition.

discoid lupus: A type of lupus that affects only the skin.

disease: An adverse change in health. Some physicians use this term only for conditions in which a structural or functional change in tissues or organs has been identified.

disease-modifying antirheumatic drugs (DMARDs): Medications used to slow or perhaps halt the progression of disease. DMARDs are used primarily to treat rheumatoid arthritis (juvenile or adult), but may also be prescribed for other inflammatory diseases such as lupus, ankylosing spondylitis and Sjögren's syndrome.

distal: Farthest from a particular point of reference.

electromyogram (EMG): A test that measures electrical activity in the muscles. This procedure is used in the diagnosis of muscle and nerve disorders.

erythema: Inflammatory redness of the skin.

erythrocyte sedimentation rate (or sed rate): A blood test that measures how quickly red blood cells cling together, fall and settle toward the bottom of a glass tube. When inflammation is present, the red blood cells settle more quickly. As inflammation responds to medication, the sed rate usually goes down.

esophageal dysmotility: Difficulty with movement of food and liquids through the esophagus.

fibromyalgia: A noninflammatory rheumatic condition affecting the body's soft tissues. Characterized by muscle pain, fatigue and non-restorative sleep, fibromyalgia has no associated abnormal X-ray or laboratory findings. It is often associated with headaches and irritable bowel syndrome.

flare: The term used to describe a period during which disease symptoms reappear or become worse.

gastroenterologist: A physician who specializes in the diagnosis, treatment and prevention of diseases of the digestive tract.

glucocorticoids: A group of powerful medications related to the natural hormones cortisone and hydrocortisone. These potent drugs quickly reduce pain and inflammation but carry a risk of serious side effects when used in high doses. Sometimes referred to as corticosteroids or steroids, they are not the same as anabolic steroid drugs that some athletes abuse.

hemoglobin: The component of blood that carries oxygen to the tissues and carbon dioxide from the tissues to the lungs for exhalation.

HLA-B27 typing: A blood test to determine if the HLA-B27 gene is present. This gene is a genetic marker associated with an increased risk of developing ankylosing spondylitis or Reiter's syndrome.

immune response: Activation of the body's immune system to defend itself against foreign substances, or antigens.

immune system: Your body's complex biochemical system for defending itself against bacteria, viruses, wounds and other injuries. Among the many components of the system are a variety of cells (such as T cells), organs (such as the lymph glands) and chemicals (such as histamine and prostaglandins).

inflammation: A reaction to injury or infection resulting in redness, pain, swelling and stiffness in the affected area.

internist: A physician who specializes in internal medicine; sometimes called a primary care physician.

iridocyclitis (iritis, uveitis): A serious eye inflammation that is difficult to detect. Permanent eye damage can be avoided by having regular eye exams by an ophthalmologist. The term an eye doctor uses to refer to the condition depends on which part of the eye is affected.

joint replacement surgery: Surgery in which diseased joints are replaced with man-made joints. This procedure is used mainly in older children and adults whose growth is complete and whose joints are badly damaged by arthritis.

juvenile ankylosing spondylitis: An inflammation of the joints of the spine as well as hips, knees and ankles that can cause the bones to fuse, or grow together. Areas where the tendons attach to bones, such as the heel bone, can become very tender as well.

juvenile dermatomyositis (JDMS): An inflammatory disease that causes a skin rash and muscle weakness. Approximately 20 percent of children with JDMS have arthritis. JDMS is more common in girls and occurs most often in children between the ages of 5 and 14.

juvenile rheumatoid arthritis (JRA): A chronic, inflammatory autoimmune disease in which the body's protective immune system attacks its own tissues, particularly the joints, causing pain, swelling and deformity. JRA is the most common type of arthritis that affects children, and there are three forms of the condition:

- **polyarticular:** Affects five or more joints, usually affecting the same joint on both sides of the body. Affects girls more often than boys.

- **pauciarticular:** Affects four or fewer joints, usually the large joints such as knees, ankles or elbows.

- **systemic onset:** Affects both the joints and internal organs, and can begin with a very high fever, rash, swollen joints and pain. This is the least common form of JRA.

leukopenia: A reduction in white blood cell count.

Lyme disease: A inflammatory disorder characterized by a skin rash, followed in weeks or months by symptoms in the central nervous system, cardiovascular system and joints. It is caused by the bite of an infected deer tick. The disease is named after the Connecticut town where it was first discovered. It is now found all across the United States.

malar rash: A rash appearing on the cheeks; also called a "butterfly rash" because of its shape. It is a common symptom of lupus.

mixed connective tissue disease (MCTD): A syndrome with a mixture of symptoms of systemic lupus erythematosus, polymyositis and other rheumatic diseases. MCTD is very rare in children.

myofascial pain syndrome: A neuromuscular condition in which the tissue surrounding muscles tightens and loses elasticity, causing pain and loss of motion.

myopathy: Any disease of a muscle.

myositis: Inflammation of a muscle. This term describes several different illnesses, including polymyositis, dermatomyositis and inclusion body myositis. These conditions involve chronic muscle inflammation, leading to muscle weakness.

nephrologist: A physician who specializes in the diagnosis, treatment and prevention of kidney problems.

neurologist: A physician who specializes in the diagnosis, treatment and prevention of nervous system disorders.

nonacetylated salicylates: Medications that are similar to aspirin, but have been chemically modified to be easier on the stomach and kidneys and are taken less frequently than regular aspirin.

nonsteroidal anti-inflammatory drugs (NSAIDs): Medications that relieve pain, fever and inflammation by blocking production of hormone-like substances called prostaglandins. These are often the first line of defense against most forms of arthritis.

nurse: A health-care practitioner who is licensed and trained to administer a variety of medical services in the treatment of illness.

occupational therapist: A health professional who teaches patients ways to reduce strain on joints while performing everyday activities. Occupational therapists also fit patients with splints and other devices to help reduce strain on joints.

oncogenesis: Development of a new abnormal growth or tumor.

ophthalmologist: A physician who specializes in the diagnosis and medical and surgical treatment of diseases and defects of the eye.

orthopaedic surgeon: A surgeon who specializes in surgery of the musculoskeletal system, its joints and related structures.

osteoporosis: A condition resulting in the thinning of bones and an increased susceptibility to fractures.

parotid gland: A gland situated near the ear that may be affected by some types of rheumatic disease.

pediatric rheumatologist: A physician who has special training in the care of children and adolescents with arthritis and related conditions.

pediatrician: A physician who has special training in the diagnosis, treatment and prevention of childhood and adolescent illnesses.

pedorthist: A person skilled in the design, modification and fit of shoes and foot appliances specifically for people with disabling conditions of the foot.

photosensitivity: An abnormally heightened reaction to sunlight.

physiatrist: A physician who specializes in the field of physical medicine and rehabilitation.

physical therapist: A licensed health professional who is a specialist in the use of exercises to treat physical conditions.

podiatrist: A health professional who specializes in the study and care of the foot, including medical and surgical treatment. Formerly called a chiropodist.

polymyositis/dermatomyositis: Related rheumatic diseases that cause weakness and inflammation of muscles.

proximal: Nearest; closest to any point of reference. (The opposite of distal.)

psoriasis: A chronic skin disease characterized by scaly, reddish patches. Psoriasis also causes lifting of the nails and pitting, a condition in which the nails become marked with several small depressions.

psoriatic arthritis: A type of arthritis that may occur with the skin condition psoriasis. Skin symptoms in children include nail pitting or ridging, and an atypical rash behind the ears, on the eyelids, elbows, knees and at the scalp line or the umbilicus. Arthritis may involve both large and small joints, usually asymetrically; the spine may also be involved.

psychiatrist: A medical doctor who specializes in the study, treatment and prevention of mental disorders. A psychiatrist may provide counseling and prescribe medicines and other therapies.

psychologist: A trained professional, usually a PhD rather than an MD, who specializes in the mind and mental processes. A psychologist may measure mental abilities and provide counseling.

pulmonologist: A physician who specializes in the diagnosis, treatment and prevention of lung disorders.

Raynaud's phenomenon: An extreme sensitivity to cold that causes narrowing of the blood vesesels in the fingers along with a sensation of burning, tingling or numbness.

reactive arthritis: A form of arthritis that develops as a reaction to certain types of infections.

Reiter's syndrome: An inflammatory condition of the joints that often follows severe intestinal or urinary tract infections. It may cause inflammation of the urinary tract, inflammation of the eyelids, mouth ulcers, and/or a skin rash. It usually develops as a reactive arthritis after *Shigella-*, *Salmonella-* or *Yersinia*-associated diarrhea.

remission: A period of time when the symptoms of a disease or condition improve or even disappear altogether.

Reye's syndrome: A rare, serious condition that sometimes occurs in children who have the chicken pox or flu and are taking aspirin. Symptoms include frequent vomiting, very painful headaches, unusual behavior, extreme tiredness and disorientation.

rheumatic diseases: A general term referring to conditions characterized by pain and stiffness of the joints or muscles. The American College of Rheumatology currently recognizes more than 100 rheumatic diseases. The term is often used interchangeably with "arthritis", but not all rheumatic diseases affect the joints or involve inflammation.

rheumatoid factor (RF): An antibody that appears in unusually high amounts in the blood of many people with rheumatoid arthritis.

rheumatoid factor (RF) test: A test to detect rheumatoid factor in the blood. Often, the higher the concentration of RF, the more severe the rheumatoid arthritis.

rheumatologist: A physician who specializes in the diagnosis, treatment and prevention of arthritis and other rheumatic disorders.

sclerodactyly: Localized scleroderma of the fingers or toes.

scleroderma: A chronic hardening and thickening of the skin. Scleroderma is rare in children. There are two general categories of scleroderma: localized scleroderma, which mainly affects the skin, and systemic scleroderma (sclerosis), which may affect the skin as well as other parts of the body.

seronegative enthesopathy and arthropathy syndrome (SEA syndrome): One of the spondyloarthropathy diseases.

social worker: A licensed professional who assists people in need by helping them capitalize on their own resources and connecting them with social services such as home nursing care or vocational rehabilitation.

soft tissue release: Surgery in which tight tissues are cut and repaired to allow the joint to return to its normal position. This type of surgery is sometimes necessary for carpal tunnel syndrome and shoulder impingement.

spondyloarthropathies: A group of diseases that involve the spine. These include ankylosing spondylitis, seronegative enthesopathy and arthropathy syndrome (SEA syndrome), arthritis associated with inflammatory bowel disease, reactive arthritis and Reiter's syndrome. These diseases occur more often in males than females.

synovectomy: Surgery in which the diseased lining of the joint, the synovial membrane, is removed.

systemic lupus erythematosus (SLE or lupus): A rheumatic disease involving the skin, joints, muscles and sometimes internal organs. Lupus is a chronic inflammatory disease characterized by fever and rash that come and go. Most children with lupus develop the disease during adolescence.

telangiectasia: Permanent dilation of blood vessels that creates small red lesions in the skin or mucous memberanes.

temporomandibular joint (TMJ): The joint in front of the ears, where the lower jaw connects to the base of the skull. Arthritis may affect this joint in the same way it does others, by causing pain, stiffness and altered growth.

thrombocytopenia: A decrease in the number of blood platelets.

vasculitis: Diseases characterized by inflammation of the blood vessels. Forms of vasculitis include Henöch-Schönlein purpura (HSP), polyarteritis nodosa, Kawasaki disease, Wegener's granulomatosis, Takayasu's arteritis, and Behçet's syndrome. These conditions can be primary childhood diseases or features of other syndromes such as juvenile dermatomyositis and lupus.

The Arthritis Foundation

The Arthritis Foundation is the source of help and hope for the estimated 43 million Americans who have arthritis and related diseases and conditions. Founded in 1948, the Arthritis Foundation is the only national, voluntary health organization that works for all people affected by any of the more than 100 forms of arthritis or related diseases. Volunteers in local offices nationwide help to support research, professional and community education programs, services for people with arthritis, government advocacy, and fund-raising activities.

The focus of the Arthritis Foundation is twofold: to support research to find the cure for and prevention of arthritis, and to improve the quality of life for those affected by arthritis. Public contributions enable the Arthritis Foundation to fulfill this mission – in fact, at least 80 cents of every dollar donated to the Arthritis Foundation serves to directly fund research and program services.

To learn more about the Arthritis Foundation, and to find a local office near you, call 800/283-7800.

American Juvenile Arthritis Organization

A council of the Arthritis Foundation, AJAO is a volunteer organization devoted to serving the special needs of children, teens and young adults with childhood rheumatic diseases. Its members are parents, family members, doctors, nurses, occupational and physical therapists, social workers, young adults, and anyone with an interest in arthritis in young people.

For more information about any of the AJAO-related services or educational materials listed below, call 404/872-7100 extension 6277.

AJAO helps members deal with the issue of childhood arthritis on many fronts. Its services include:

Support – AJAO groups in many Arthritis Foundation chapters and local offices allow members to exchange ideas, encouragement and friendship.

Information – AJAO serves as a clearinghouse of information for the public on topics from medications, educational rights and social services to legislative issues. In addition, AJAO publishes a quarterly membership newsletter and other educational materials.

Conferences – AJAO sponsors national and regional conferences for children and families. These conferences provide education, support, fun and games for all members of the family.

Advocacy – AJAO monitors and promotes legislation that affects children with arthritis.

Research – The Arthritis Foundation sponsors research into the causes of adult and juvenile arthritis. It also strongly supports the federally funded National Institute of Arthritis, Musculoskeletal and Skin Diseases.

Training – Through the Partnership Training Program, AJAO trains parents and health professionals to promote education rights, family support and care coordination for children with arthritis in their own communities.

Awards – AJAO honors parents, young people, and health professionals who have shown exceptional strength and leadership in dealing with juvenile arthritis.

Educational Materials

Additional information and links to other resources are available on the Arthritis Foundation's World Wide Web page: **http:\\www.arthritis.org.**

General Information

Arthritis Today (bimonthly magazine) – National consumer magazine with news about arthritis research, treatments and coping tips.

Arthritis Answers – A booklet describing the different forms of arthritis and the most common treatments.

Kids Get Arthritis, Too – A booklet that describes AJAO and includes membership information.

AJAO Newsletter – Provides current information about issues affecting children with rheumatic diseases. Available to AJAO members.

Americans with Disabilities Act Resource Guide – Step-by-step information on obtaining benefits.

Arthritis in Children – A booklet giving medical information about juvenile rheumatoid arthritis for parents or other adults, describing the illness, medication, therapies and coping.

Arthritis and Pregnancy – A booklet about how arthritis affects pregnancy; includes tips on managing a pregnancy and a new baby.

Drug Guide – Describes how medicines work, how to take them and possible side effects.

<u>Medication booklets:</u>
Penicillamine
Corticosteroid Medications
Gold Treatment
Hydroxychloroquine
Methotrexate

For Children
Yard Sale (booklet) – Story and coloring book about two girls who become friends; one of them has arthritis. Based on the Kids on the Block, Inc. arthritis puppet program. Ages 4-10.

Shake, Rattle & Roar! – This 20-minute Arthritis Foundation exercise videotape uses a zoo theme to lead children through exercises designed for children with and without physical limitations. An accompanying lesson plan guide is included for teachers of children from kindergarten through second grade.

For Young Adults

Decision Making for Teenagers with Arthritis – A booklet to help teens make career and higher education choices.

Arthritis in the Workplace – A booklet explaining workplace and hiring rights, as well as ways to adapt your work environment.

Young Adult Connection – A package of information for use in helping address the needs of young adults with arthritis, ages 18-44.

School

Educational Rights for Children with Arthritis: A Manual for Parents – A book that educates parents of children with arthritis about how to obtain services and accommodations for their children in school.

When Your Student Has Arthritis: A Guide for Teachers – A booklet for teachers or other adults who know children with arthritis. Describes different forms of juvenile arthritis, how arthritis might affect a child at school and how to help.

Services

AJAO Resource Catalog – Describes printed materials, video cassettes and slide and tape programs of various forms of juvenile arthritis not produced by the Arthritis Foundation.

Partnership Training Workshops – Three workshops for parents and health professionals: one on educational rights of students with arthritis; one on family support; one on care coordination. Please call your local Arthritis Foundation office for workshop listings.

American Juvenile Arthritis Organization (AJAO)
Arthritis Foundation National Office
1330 West Peachtree St., NW
Atlanta, GA 30309
(404) 872-7100 extension 6277
(800) 283-7800
www.arthritis.org

Other Arthritis Foundation Offerings

Along with the programs, services and information designed for children and families of those with arthritis, The Arthritis Foundation offers a variety of programs and services for adults with arthritis. These services include physician referral, land and aquatic exercise programs, exercise videotapes, support and education groups, self-help courses, and brochures, books and periodicals. To find out more about the services for adults that the Foundation offers, call your local office.

Remember the Arthritis Foundation in Your Will

Planned giving is an important part of fulfilling the Arthritis Foundation's mission to support research and improve the quality of life for those affected by arthritis. The Arthritis Foundation offers a wide variety of gift planning options – gifts of cash, appreciated assets, gifts by will or living trust, naming the Arthritis Foundation as beneficiary of your life insurance, individual retirement account, pension, 401(k), or other retirement savings plan.

It is our hope that you decide to include a gift to the Arthritis Foundation in your will. Your greatest benefit in assisting the Arthritis Foundation will be the personal satisfaction of making a difference in the struggle against arthritis. For more information on giving opportunities, call the planned giving department at 404/872-7100.

BIBLIOGRAPHY

Cassidy JT, Petty RE. *Textbook of Pediatric Rheumatology*, Third Edition, W.B. Saunders Company, Philadelphia, 1995.

Klippel JH, Weyand CM, Wortmann RL. *Primer on the Rheumatic Diseases*, Edition 11. Arthritis Foundation, Atlanta, 1997.

Dunkin MA. Drug guide. Arthritis Today. July-August, 1997.

Arthritis in Children. Arthritis Foundation, 1996.

Brewer EJ, Angel KC. *Parenting a Child with Arthritis*. Lowell House, Los Angeles, 1995.

Brand names of drugs are in *italics*.

Abdominal exercises, 58
Acetaminophen, 33
Acetylated salicylates, 31
Acting out, of negative feelings, 114
Activity. *See also* Exercises
    charts for daily, 98
    depression and decreases in, 67
    group, 62
    importance of daily, 27
    pain or stiffness interference with, 18
    solo, 62
Actron, 30
ADA (Americans with Disabilities Act) (1990),
    139–140, 156
Adherence monitoring, in treatment, 99, 102
Adolescents. *See* Teenagers
Advil, 30
Advocacy, for children with arthritis
    American Juvenile Arthritis Organization and,
        159
    Arthritis Foundation and, 158
    parents and, 158
    strategies for, 159
Age, of disease onset
    effect of, 114
    of juvenile dermatomyositis, 10
    of juvenile systemic lupus erythematosus, 8
AJAO. *See* American Juvenile Arthritis Organization
    (AJAO)
Alcohol, arthritis and, 32, 146
Alternative treatments
    considerations in, 74–76
    precautions for, 23
American Juvenile Arthritis Organization (AJAO), 4
    about, 110, 179
    address of, 183
    advocacy work and, 159
    Arthritis Awareness Week and, 125–126
    pen pal program of, 117
    as resource source, 179–182
    support for medical cost control, 158
Americans with Disabilities Act (ADA) (1990),
    139–140, 156
ANA (antinuclear antibodies), 92
Anacin, 31
Anemia, 88
Ankle exercises, 51, 61
Ansaid, 30

Antinuclear antibodies (ANA), 92
Arm exercises, 61
Arthritis
    definitions of, 3–4
    juvenile (*see* Juvenile arthritis (JA))
Arthritis Foundation, 110
    advocacy efforts of, 158
    assistance in finding camps, 118
    assistance in finding physicians, 17
    on eligibility standards for medical service
        programs, 159
    information assistance from, 23
    pamphlets for teachers from, 123
    as resource source, 179–183
Arthroscopic surgery, 78
Ascriptin, 31
Aspirin, 30–31
Autoantibodies, in mixed connective tissue
    disease, 11
Azathioprine, 31, 32
Azulfidine, 31

Back exercises, 48, 58
Bacterial infections, arthritis and, 8
Balanced Budget Act (1997), 152
Ballet, 61
Baths
    in pain relief, 70
    tips for, 85
Bathtub play, 60
Bayer, 31
Behçet's syndrome, 10
Bicycling, 59
Biologic therapies, 33
Blood tests, 8, 17, 77
Body Outline for Pain, 164–165
Bones, 88, 90
Bone scans, 78
Bufferin, 31

Caffeine, 72
Calcium
    medications and, 88, 90
    side effects of glucocorticoids and, 32
    sources of, 90–91
Camps, locating and evaluating, 118
Career interests, determining, 138–140
Chairs, 53
Checklists, for school needs, 128–131
Chest and shoulders, posture and, 56–57

Child care, finding, 108, 111

Child Care and Development Block Grant, 157

Child development stages

    age 2 to 3, 114

    age 4 to 6, 115

    age 7 to 11, 115

    age 12 to 15, 116

    age 16 to 19, 116

    infancy, 114

Children's Hospital Medical Center (University of Cincinnati), 155

Children's Medical Services (CMS), 159

Children's Special Health-Care Services, 152

Children with Special Health Care Needs, 159

Chores, 104–105

Clinoril, 30

CMS (Children's Medical Services), 159

Cold treatments, in pain relief, 72

College

    attendant assistance in, 144–145

    general issues in selection of, 141–142

    getting the most from, 143–144

    paying for, 146–147

    physical issues in selection of, 142

    preparing for admission tests for, 140–141

    residential issues in, 144–146

    special issues in selection of, 142

    tips for avoiding overload in, 143–144

Communication

    child, with health-care professionals, 19, 80, 116

    in family, 109

    parental, with health-care professionals, 15–18, 80, 81

Complaints, handling of child's, 100

Complementary treatments, 75, 76

Compliance monitoring, in treatment, 99

Contractures (frozen joints), 37–38, 54, 78

Coping

    with child's chronic illness, 105

    with pain with self-talk, 68

    with teasing, 117, 125

Corticosteroids. *See* Glucocorticoids

Cortisone, 32

Costs, of treatment, 19, 35. *See also* Financial issues

CREST syndrome, 11

Cutaneous polyarteritis, 10

Cyclophosphamide, 31

Cyclosporine, 31

Daily living. *See also* Diet

    bathing and grooming, 84–85

    dental care, 92–93

    dressing, 85–86, 135

    eating, 86

    eye care, 92

    joint protection, 83–84

    posture in, 84

Dancing, 60, 61

Daypro, 30

Deductions, medical, 151

Dental care, 92–93

Depression

    chronic pain and, 66–67

    parental, 108

Dermatomyositis. *See* Juvenile dermatomyositis (JDMS)

Dexamethasone, 32

Diagnosis, of arthritis, 4–5

Diclofenac sodium, 30

Diet. *See also* Calcium

    fad, 88

    during flares, 88–89

    folic acid in, 32, 88

    Food Guide Pyramid, 87

    snacks in, 88

    sodium in, 88

    vitamin D in, 32, 91

Disalcid, 31

Discipline, for child with chronic disease, 100–101

Disease-modifying antirheumatic drugs (DMARDs), 31–32

Dressing, tips for, 85–86, 135

Drinking, arthritis and, 32, 146

Drug interactions, 34

Eating, tips for, 86. *See also* Diet

Ecotrin, 31

Education. *See also* School

    about arthritis, 4

    entitlements in, 156–157

Education for All Handicapped Children Act, Amendment (1986), 156

Education for All Handicapped Children Act (1975), 156

Elbow exercises, 44

Electric blankets, in pain relief, 71

Endorphins, 63, 66

Endurance exercises, 39

Energy, conservation of child's physical, 72–73

Entitlements, in education, 156–157
Erythema nodosum, 12
Etodolac, 30
Excedrin, 31
Exercises. *See also* Posture; *specific sports*
    abdominal, 58
    ankle, 51, 61
    arm, 61
    back, 48, 58
    elbow, 44
    fingers, 46–47
    guidelines for performing, 39–40
    hand, 61
    hip, 47, 49–50
    importance of daily, 37–38
    knee, 47, 52
    leg, 48, 52–53, 61
    neck, 41–42
    shoulder, 42–43, 56–57
    types of, 39
    when to do, 38–39
    wrist, 45–46
Eyes
    care of, 92
    inflammation of, 7, 33
    medication-related damage of, 31

Fad diets, 88
Family
    child care for, 111
    communication in, 109
    dealing with feelings, 105
    parental marriage, 108
    positive self-image encouragement by,
        104–105, 115
    rain check planning by, 103–104
    siblings, 106–107
    support during medical visits, 17
    vacations, tips for, 111–112
FDA (Food and Drug Administration), 29
Feet, 56, 61
Feldene, 30
Fenoprofen calcium, 30
Fibromyalgia syndrome, primary, 12–13
Financial issues. *See also* Costs, of treatment
    federal programs, 151–152
    health insurance, 149–151
    state programs, 152–153
    tips for medical expenses, 151
Finger exercises, 46–47

Flares
    definition of, 39, 75
    diet during, 88–89
    exercise during, 38–39
Flurbiprofen, 30
Folic acid, 32, 88
Food and Drug Administration (FDA), 29
Food Guide Pyramid, 87
Foot exercises, 61
Friendships, 117
Frozen joints (contractures), 37–38, 54, 78

Games
    kicking balls, 61
    "red light/green light," 61
    "Simon Says," 40, 60
    tag, 61
Gender
    benign hypermobility syndromes and, 12
    juvenile arthritis incidence and, ix
    juvenile dermatomyositis and, 10
    juvenile rheumatoid arthritis incidence and, 7
    juvenile spondyloarthropathy incidence and, 8
    Kawasaki disease incidence and, 10
Generic medications, 19, 35. *See also* Medications
Glossary, 170–178
Glucocorticoids, 32–33, 88, 90, 115
Gold compounds, 31–32
Grooming, tips for, 84–85
Growing pains, 12

Hand exercises, 61
Handwriting, tips for difficulties with, 135
Head Start Act, 157
Health-care professionals
    child communication with, 19, 80, 116
    choosing, 16–17
    numbers of different, 4, 15
    numbers of pediatric rheumatologists, 157
    parental communication with, 15–18, 80, 81
    on play and recreational activities, 60
    second opinions and, 22
Health history, 4
Health Maintenance Organizations (HMOs), 150
Health plans, traditional, 150
Heat treatments, in pain relief, 38, 70–71, 98
Henöch-Schönlein purpura (HSP), 10
Hip exercises, 47, 49–50
HLA-B27 blood tests, 8
HMOs (Health Maintenance Organizations), 150

Hospitalization, 80–82

Hot packs, in pain relief, 70

HSP (Henöch-Schönlein purpura), 10

Hydrocollator packs, 70

Hydrocortisone, 32

Hydroxychloroquine sulfate, 31

Hypermobility syndromes, benign, 12

Ibuprofen, 30

Ice skating, 61

IDEA. *See* Individuals with Disabilities Education
    Act (IDEA) (PL 94-142)

IEP (Individualized Education Plan), 124, 141

Illnesses, childhood, medications and, 35

Immunoglobulins, intravenous (IVIG), 33

Imuran, 32

Individualized Education Plan (IEP), 124, 141

Individuals with Disabilities Education Act (IDEA)
    (PL 94-142), 123, 156, 157

Individuals with Disabilities Education Act (IDEA)
    (PL 94-142), re-authorization 1997, 156

Indocin, 30

Indomethacin, 30

Inflammation
    of eyes, 7, 33
    of skin, 33

Insurance, health, 152
    comprehensive, 149
    managed care plans, 149–150
    selection of, 150–151

Iridocyclitis, in juvenile rheumatoid arthritis, 7
    See also Eyes

IVIG (intravenous immunoglobulins), 33

JA. *See* Juvenile arthritis (JA)

Jaycees, 153

JDMS (juvenile dermatomyositis), 9–10

Jobs, summer and part-time, 139

Joint fluid tests, 5, 78

Joint injection, 78

Joint replacement surgery, 78–79

Joints
    frozen, 37–38, 78
    protection of, 83–84
    splinting, 74

JRA. *See* Juvenile rheumatoid arthritis (JRA)

Juvenile ankylosing spondylitis, 8

Juvenile Arthritis Awareness Week, 125–126

Juvenile arthritis (JA). *See also specific types*
    diagnosis and features of, 4–5

forms of, 3

incidence of, ix

numbers of children with, 3

types of, 5–13

understanding of, 27

Juvenile dermatomyositis (JDMS), 9–10

Juvenile psoriatic arthritis, 8

Juvenile rheumatoid arthritis (JRA)
    features of, 5–6
    pauciarticular, 5, 6–7
    polyarticular, 5, 6
    systemic, 7
    types of, 5

Juvenile sclerodermas
    localized, 10–11
    systemic, 11

Juvenile spondyloarthropathy syndromes, 8

Juvenile systemic lupus erythematosus (SLE), 8–9

Juvenile vasculitis, 10

Kawasaki disease, 10

Ketoprofen, 30

Ketorolac, 30

Kids' Care Insurance, 152

Kiwanis, 153

Knee exercises, 47, 52

Laboratory tests, 5
    blood, 8, 17, 77
    joint fluid, 5, 78
    urine, 77
    X-ray examinations, 5, 78

Leg exercises, 48, 52–53, 61

Lifestyle. *See* Daily living

Linear scleroderma, 11

Lodine, 30

Lupus. *See* Systemic lupus erythematosus (SLE)

Marriage, child's arthritis effect on parental, 108

Maternal and Child Health office, federal, 155

Maternal and Child Health Services Block
    Grant, 157

Mattresses, 53, 71

Mattress pads, in pain relief, 71

MCTD (mixed connective tissue disease), 11–12

Meclofenamate sodium, 30

Meclomen, 30

Medicaid Supplemental Care Assistance, 152

Medical records, 17, 22

Medical visits, getting the most from. *See also*

Health-care professionals
after the visit, 22–23
questions to ask doctor, 21
things to tell doctor, 20
before the visit, 16–17
during the visit, 17–21
Medicare, 152
Medications. *See also* Side effects, of medications
after surgery, 80
analgesics, 33
biologic therapies, 33
costs of, 35
diet and, 88, 90
disease-modifying antirheumatic drugs, 31–32
generic, 19, 35
glucocorticoids, 32–33, 115
goals of, 30
guidelines for, 33–35
keeping track of, 17
nonsteroidal anti-inflammatory drugs, 30
pamphlets on, 181
questions about, 34
salicylates, 30–31
Methotrexate, 31, 32, 90
Methylprednisolone, 32
Mixed connective tissue disease (MCTD), 11–12
Morphea, 11
Motrin, 30
Motrin IB, 30
Myochrysine, 31

Nabumetone, 30
Nalfon, 30
Naprosyn, 30
Naproxen, 30
National Institute of Arthritis, Musculoskeletal and
Skin Diseases grants, 155
Neck exercises, 41–42
Neonatal systemic lupus erythematosus, 9
Nonacetylated salicylates, 31
Non-inflammatory disorders, forms of, 3, 12–13
Nonsteroidal anti-inflammatory drugs (NSAIDS), 30
Note taking
before medical visits, 17
during medical visits, 18
NSAIDs (nonsteroidal anti-inflammatory drugs), 30
Nuprin, 30
Nutrition. *See* Diet

Orudis, 30
Orudis KT, 30
Oruvail, 30
Osteoporosis, 88, 90
Overlap syndromes, 11
Overuse syndromes, 13
Overweight, 88
Oxaprozin, 30

Pain
behaviors associated with, 68
beliefs about, 67–68
cautions in management of, 64
chronic, 64, 66–67
consequences of, 67
coping self-talk and, 68
definition of, 63–64, 66
depression and chronic, 66–67
descriptions of, 17, 164–165
effect on school performance, 125
evaluation of, 162–163
parental responses to, 68
perception of, 64–65
understanding, 63–65
Pain puzzle concept, 66–68
Pain relief. *See also* Medications
after surgery, 80
cold treatments in, 72
heat treatments in, 38, 70–71, 98
positive thinking in, 69
relaxation techniques in, 69–70
safety tips in, 72
Pain syndromes, 12–13
Panniculitis, 12
Paraffin baths, in pain relief, 70–71
Parents
as children's rights advocates, 158
communication with health-care professionals,
15–18, 80, 81
coping with child's chronic illness, 105
depression and, 108
impact of arthritis diagnosis on marriage of, 108
responses to child's pain, 68
responsibilities in treatment, 23, 97
single, 109–110
support for, 110
Parents' groups, 110
Pauciarticular juvenile rheumatoid arthritis,
5, 6–7, 92

Pediapred, 32

Pelvis-abdomen, posture and, 58

Penicillamine, 31

Pen pal program, 117

Physical activity. *See* Activity; Exercises; Play and
 recreational activities; Posture

Physical education, 62, 125

Physical education activity guide, 132–133

Physical examination, 4

Physicians, choosing, 16–17

Pillows, 53

Piroxicam, 30

Plaquenil, 31

Play and recreational activities
 for older children and teenagers, 61–62
 restrictions and guidelines for, 59–60
 for young children, 60–61

Point of Service (POS) Plan, 150

Polyarteritis nodosa, 10

Polyarticular juvenile rheumatoid arthritis, 5, 6

Positive thinking, in pain relief, 69

POS (Point of Service Plan), 150

Posture. *See also* Exercise
 chest and shoulders, 56–57
 correct reclining, 55
 correct sitting, 55, 134
 correct standing, 54
 in daily living, 84
 development of good, 56–59
 pelvis-abdomen, 58
 upper back, 58

PPO (Preferred Provider Organization), 150

Prednisone, 32

Preferred Provider Organization (PPO), 150

Prelone, 32

Preventive measures, 19

Psoriatic arthritis (juvenile psoriatic arthritis), 8

Quilts, in pain relief, 71

Range of motion exercises, 39, 40. *See also* Exercises

Rapoff, Michael, 65

Raynaud's phenomenon, 11

Reclining posture, 55

Recreational activities. *See* Play and recreational
 activities

Reflex sympathetic dystrophy (RSD), 13

Rehabilitation Act (1973), Section 504, 156

Reiter's syndrome, 8

Relafen, 30

Relaxation techniques, in pain relief, 69–70

Remission, 75

Research centers, 155

Resources, for arthritis patients and families. *See
 also* American Juvenile Arthritis Organization
 (AJAO); Arthritis Foundation
 for children, 181
 general information, 180–181
 medication pamphlets, 181
 on school-related programs, 182
 on services, 182
 for young adults, 182

Respite care, 108

Reye's syndrome, 31

Rheumatic diseases in childhood, classification of,
 166–169

Rheumatoid arthritis. *See* Juvenile rheumatoid
 arthritis (JRA)

Rheumatology centers, 155

Rheumatrex, 32

Ridaura, 31

Rights, in education, 156–157

Roller skating, 61

RSD (reflex sympathetic dystrophy), 13

Salicylates, 30–31

Salmonella spp., 8

Sandimmune, 32

School
 common concerns about, 134–135
 daily living activities for, 83–84
 educating, about arthritis, 123, 124–126
 entitlements for, 156–158
 needs checklist for, 128–131
 physical education in, 62, 125, 132–133

Sclerodermas, juvenile, 10–11

Second opinions, 22

Self-image, encouragement of positive, 104–105, 115

Self-talk, coping with pain via, 68

Sexuality, 118

Shigella spp., 8

Shoes, good posture and, 56

Shoulder exercises, 42–43, 56–57
 abduction, 43
 rotation, 43

Shriners, 153

Siblings, of child with arthritis, 106–107

Sicca syndrome, 12

Side effects, of medications
 azathioprine, 32

cyclosporine, 32
glucocorticoids, 32, 88, 90, 115
gold compounds, 32
hydroxychloroquine sulfate, 31
immunoglobulins, intravenous, 33
minimizing, 98–99
nonsteroidal anti-inflammatory drugs, 30
salicylates, 31
stomach irritation, 99
sulfasalazine, 32
Single parents, 109–110
Sitting posture, 55, 134
Sjögren's syndrome, primary, 11–12
Skills assessment, 138–139
Skin inflammation, 33
Sleep, tips for, 72–73
SLE (systemic lupus erythematosus), 8–9
Snacks, 88
Social adjustment
    encouraging positive self-image for, 104–105
    rain check planning and, 103–104
Social Security Act, Title V, 155
Social Security Disability Insurance (SSDI or Title II),
    152
Sodium, 88
Solganol, 31
Special education programs, 123–124
Splints, 74
Spondylitis, juvenile ankylosing, 8
Spondyloarthropathy syndromes, juvenile, 8
SSDI (Social Security Disability Insurance), 152
SSI (Supplemental Security Income), 151
Stages, of childhood. *See* Child development stages
Stairs, tips for dealing with, 134
Standing posture, 54
Stay-in-School Program, 140
Steroids. *See* Glucocorticoids
Stomach irritation, as side effect of medications, 99
Strengthening exercises, 39
Stress management, 105, 108
Sulfasalazine, 31
Sulindac, 30
Summer Aid Program, 140
Sun protection, in systemic lupus erythematosus, 9
Supplemental Security Income (SSI or
    Title XVI), 151
Surgery
    preparing child for, 80–82
    questions to ask about, 79
    types of, 78

Swallowing, difficulties with, 35
Swimming, 59, 61
Symptoms, discussions with doctor about, 18.
    See also specific diseases
Synovectomy, 78
Systemic juvenile rheumatoid arthritis, 7
Systemic lupus erythematosus, juvenile (SLE), 8–9
Systemic sclerosis (scleroderma), 11

Takayasu's arteritis, 10
Taxes, medical deductions and, 151
Teachers. *See also* School
    educating about arthritis, 123, 124–126
    sample letter to, 126–127
Team sports, 62
Teasing, coping with, 117, 125
Teenagers
    adherence monitoring and, 99
    college and (*see* College)
    development of, 116
    drinking and drugs and, 146
    recreational activities for, 61–62
    sexuality and, 118
    skills assessment by, 138–139
    summer and part-time jobs and, 139
Temporomandibular joint, 92
Therapeutic play, 81
Title II (Social Security Disability Insurance), 152
Title V, Social Security Act, 155
Title XVI (Supplemental Security Income), 151
Tolectin, 30
Tolmetin sodium, 30
Toradol, 30
Tramadol, 33
Treatment. *See also* Pain relief
    adherence monitoring in, 99, 102
    alternative, 23, 74–76
    changes in, 19, 22–23
    child's responsibilities in, 22–23, 35, 115
    complementary, 75, 76
    costs of, 19, 35
    discipline needs in, 100–101
    goals and strategies for, 26–36
    health-care professionals and, 4, 16–23
    minimizing side effects of, 98–99
    parental responsibilities in, 15–18, 23, 97
    reminders for, 98, 102
    scheduling of, 98
Trilisate, 31

Ultram, 33
Upper back, posture and, 58
Urine tests, 77

Vacations, tips for, 111–112
Varni/Thompson Pediatric Pain Questionnaire,
 162–163
Vasculitis, juvenile, 10
Vitamin D
 side effects of glucocorticoids and, 32
 sources of, 91
Vocational Education Act, 157
Vocational Rehabilitation (VR) Services,
 146–147, 152
Voltaren, 30
Voluntary groups, financial assistance from, 153

Waterbeds, in pain relief, 71
Water polo, 61
Wegener's granulomatosis, 10
When Your Student Has Arthritis, 123
Wrist exercises, 45–46

X-ray examinations, 5, 78

Yersinia spp., 8